A Week in

I.S.B.N. 9781718104...

Dedication

For Mike. Twenty past eleven.

August 1978

It was my third day at secondary school and I found myself sitting at a little wooden, slope-topped desk in a strange classroom with strange writing on the walls and a Tricolour flag in one corner of the room. The lid of the desk was stuck firmly shut with countless years-worth of masticated chewing gum, and the original hole for an ink well, stained black around its edges, was now filled not with a little pot of Quink but with pencil shavings, scraps of paper and more grey, rock hard chewing gum.

The class of some twenty five girls was beginning to get a little bit rowdy when suddenly the door was flung open and a smartly dressed middle aged woman, wearing the standard twin set and pearls of all the female teaching staff, walked briskly into the room. A hush fell and into the silence, my first ever French lesson began.

"Bonjour mes enfants…" She continued to speak, in French, with barely a pause for breath, for what seemed to be several minutes.

"Oh, no," I recall my eleven year old self thinking, "she doesn't speak English! How is this ever going to work?"

Of course, Madame did speak English, and for the next three years she did her best to make sure we all spoke not just English but French too. Some of us girls went on learning French right up until we took our 'O' Level exams and left school. Some of us switched to German. I am a great believer that the best way to learn a language is to visit the country, immerse yourself in the culture, talk to the natives. And so when I reached the final two years of school and was choosing which subjects to study, and having never visited France, I dropped French and continued with German. My logic fell down a bit there as I'd never been to Germany either. In fact, I had never been abroad, but I found the more phonetic German far easier to speak and read than the language of love, of romance, of strange combinations of Cs and Qs and apostrophes. I could bark out a long winded sentence in German, with words of twelve and fifteen characters, far easier than I could purr out even a single French verb. Basically the language of harsh commands came more naturally to me than ever did the language of love.

Not that much more naturally though as time was to reveal! Fast forward to August 1983 and the exam results were published. Along with a string of good 'O' Level grades in English, maths, sciences and a couple of humanities subjects (I tell you this so you don't think I'm a complete idiot), I had a C.S.E. certificate in German. Now for those of you too young to remember education before G.C.S.E., an 'O' Level pass was the equivalent of a good G.C.S.E. grade. C.S.E.s were the lower tier, the exam you were put in for if the school thought you were a lost cause in that particular subject. I was such a lost cause I was almost off the scale. I opened the envelope with the C.S.E. certificate in and anxiously read the results: German grade four. The grading only went down to five. Dummkopf!

Today, my German is just about good enough to buy train tickets, order food, ask where the cathedral is and to swear when it all gets too much. My French however, is another matter. Three years of listening and repeating Longman's Audio Visual French, those old tape to tape spools and the books that accompanied them bring back a hint of nostalgia. Learning all about Jean-Paul, Pierre and Claudette and their chien, well, it was fun at the time. But the only thing I can recall about those French lessons is how to ask someone if they have a blue pen or a red chair, not two questions you are ever likely to need to ask; and the only two French words I can confidently pronounce are Ecouter et répéter – which was how the Longman tapes began every lesson! I am embarrassed to admit that my French language skills are on a par with Del Boy Trotter, the policeman from 'Allo 'Allo! and Peter Sellers playing Inspector Clouseau. So whenever I visit France, although I try my best, I usually rely on Mike to communicate. He, at least, has 'O' Level French.

October 2014

"You've brought how many pairs of underpants?" I was sitting on my bedroom floor, trying to cram various items of clothing for two people, toiletries and a large quantity of tea bags into one suitcase.

"Two" repeated Mike sheepishly. "I thought I'd put more in but I can't find them now."

"When I phoned you last night and you asked me what we needed to take you interrupted me when I started listing all the clothes and said you didn't need to know about that! Now you're telling me you've only got two pairs of undies for a week's holiday!"

This is the problem when (a) you live apart, (b) your partner thinks he has a mind of his own and (c) you fly with a budget airline. We had booked to fly from Liverpool to Nice with one of the cheaper airlines – you know the ones – everything comes at an additional cost. They have all the usual features of a regular airline: wings, engines, a pilot, oxygen masks in the event of an emergency (although I think you have to put a pound in the slot before the oxygen is dispensed) but they then charge for just about everything else, including hold luggage. So as we were only going on holiday for a week we had decided to economise by only taking one suitcase and thus saving ourselves £65. We would be staying in an apartment with a washing machine and so had reduced the number of clothes we were taking with the intention of washing some while we were away; I

6

just hadn't envisaged having to wash underpants every other day.

"Oh, hang on! I've found another pair!" Mike exclaimed triumphantly, delving through the holdall he had brought.

"Oh, good, three pairs of undies! Better not have an accident had you?"

With the suitcase packed, tea bags safely stowed and the lid closed, we weighed the suitcase (didn't want to incur an outrageous premium at the check-in desk) and went to bed.

Beep! Beep! Beep! The alarm clock seemed to be going off just minutes after we had gone to sleep. Three fifteen in the morning. Time to get up, we had a plane to catch. Two hours later we were unloading the car at Liverpool airport. Mike began wheeling the suitcase through the car park towards the terminal but he was struggling with the handle.

"Do you want me to wheel it?" I asked as it spun out of control for the third time.

"No, I can manage. It's just that the handle could do with being longer."

"More like your arms could do with being longer," I laughed.

"What, like yours?" Five in the morning and it's never too early to start teasing one another.

7

"What's wrong with my arms? They are proportional to my legs."

"You admitted you'd scraped your knuckles on the bottom of the swimming pool last week!"

"Yes, but the water level had dropped! The pool had a leak!" I defended myself. "Anyway you're shorter than I am, so you should be able to reach the suitcase handle more easily."

"Only half an inch!" he exclaimed indignantly (and inaccurately).

"An inch!"

I didn't catch his reply as I had spotted an abandoned luggage trolley and scurried off to retrieve it.

"Here, put the suitcase on this," I instructed, catching up with him.

"I don't need that!"

"Yes, but someone has left a pound in the slot, so I'm taking it back to the terminal to get the pound out, so you might as well use it!" I explained. Up a pound - what better way to start the holiday?

€-€-€-€-€

"Have you left your luggage unattended?" asked the lady on the check-in desk.

"No," we chorused.

"And have you got any of these items in your luggage?" she held up an A4 card with a long list of items all illustrated and labelled.

We scanned the card: shotgun, aerosol, knife, bomb with a lighted fuse hanging out of the top, can of paint.

"Who on earth takes a tin of paint on holiday with them?" I asked in astonishment.

The lady just shrugged and Mike elbowed me with embarrassment. He probably thought I was about to say something sarcastic (me?) that would result in us being marched off and strip searched.

Suitcase taken care of we ambled off and joined the security queue, ferretting about in our rucksacks to find our passports. Mike had just had his renewed, and I pulled it out of his grasp to admire the latest photograph.

"Next on the most wanted wall tonight is this character. Cumbria Constabulary is looking for this man wanted for crimes against fashion. If you see him do not approach him…" I chortled through my best Crimewatch impersonation before Mike snatched the passport back and grabbed mine.

"You've no room to talk! You look like one of the Baader-Meinhof Gang!"

9

Does anyone actually look like their passport photo? If you do, surely you're too ill to travel?

The queue of families, couples, business men and odd assorted groups slowly moved forward. A group of three later middle aged Liverpudlian women, who had been in front of us at check-in, were once again just in front of us and were in boisterous mood, chatting and screeching with laughter, and causing almost everyone in the queue to look around to see what all the commotion was about. One of the women, with startling orange hair, seemed to have forgotten to put her teeth in.

"How can you go on holiday without your teeth?" muttered Mike.

"Maybe she's broken them and can't afford any more. They're not cheap even if you have an NHS dentist."

"She can afford to fly to Nice."

"Yes but it is with a budget airline. You'd be lucky to get a filling for the same price as this flight!"

"I guess she'll be having lots of soft cheese and no baguettes," he commented.

Most of the security staff looked quite mild mannered but the woman who examined my passport was a little more threatening. I've heard of Mr Potato Head packing his angry eyes, but this woman seemed to have gone one step further, plucking out her eyebrows entirely and pencilling back on her intimidating eyebrows. I smiled nervously as her assessing gaze scanned first my passport and then my face. Perhaps she pencilled different shaped eyebrows on depending on her mood? There could be the 'come to bed' eyebrows, the 'may I help you' eyebrows, the 'pass me the latex gloves and bend over' eyebrows. After careful scrutiny she obviously thought I looked harmless and waved me on.

I don't like waiting at airports, I don't suppose anyone does. We killed time looking at the duty free, the book shops, the tie shop and the Liverpool memorabilia shop. I visited the toilets about three times, determined not to need to empty my bladder once we were on the plane.

"You can't possibly need to go again?" asked Mike at the third toilets.

"Just squeezing out every last drop."

"How much tea did you drink at breakfast?"

We sat for an hour staring at a row of vending machines, or rather Mike did, I read my book about a British woman cycling through Japan. The three women with only two sets of teeth walked past, still in high spirits.

"Keep going," I whispered sarcastically so that only Mike could hear. "There's a vending machine down there that sells teeth!"

Mike burst out laughing, asking, "What made you say that?"

"Well according to this book I'm reading, you can buy just about anything from a vending machine in Japan! Maybe even dentures!"

Our flight took off and landed on time. As soon as it touched down there was the mad scramble to empty the overhead luggage bins. We sat it out, there seemed little point rushing when we would all have to queue for passport control and then wait for the hold luggage to be unloaded.

Liverpool had been cold and damp. Nice was hot and sunny even in late October. We left the terminal, catching the shuttle bus to terminal one and then following directions to collect our hire car, not, as it turned out, from the rank of on-airport car rental firms but from a nearby hotel.

"How come we're getting the car from a hotel?" asked Mike as he wheeled the unruly suitcase across a main road and through several hotel car parks.

"Cheapest one that came up when I googled it, mon sewer."

"What?"

"It was the cheapest car hire."

"Yes, I got that bit. It was the bit about a sewer I didn't understand."

"Mon sewer: mister in French."

"Oh god," Mike rolled his eyes. "You've got the pronunciation all wrong."

At the hotel we found the car hire desk tucked into a corner of the lobby. If I had been hoping to leave all the talking to Mike I was in for a shock as the booking had been made in my name. Fortunately the man behind the counter spoke excellent English, so at least one of us did. Paperwork taken care of, he led us down into the underground garage, ran through a few safety checks, checked the car over for damage and pointed us in the direction of the exit.

I was designated driver. Mike was designated navigator. Fairly soon into our relationship, Mike became painfully aware that I'm not great with maps. A lifetime walking the Lakeland hills and two decades in Ambleside Mountain Rescue Team means Mike is excellent with maps. I'd much rather have the stresses of driving aboard than listen to him shout at me if I mess up the navigation. I say if but actually it should really be when.

So with Mike in the passenger seat surrounded by maps and directions, and me in the driver's seat surrounded by hand brakes and gear levers in the wrong place, we set off. We had hired a compact car and thank goodness we had. The underground garage was short on space and tight on turns. I inched carefully along, conscious of the €700 insurance excess that had been put on my credit card with the promise the payment would be cancelled if the vehicle came back intact. At the automatic exit barrier we left the garage, driving up a steep ramp and onto a street busy with traffic.

"Left turn," said Mike without looking up from the map.

"Ne possible pas," I replied.

"What?"

"It means 'that is not possible'," I explained.

"I know what it means. I want to know why you can't turn left."

"Because this hotel seems to be sitting in the middle of southern Europe's biggest one way system!"

"Oh, bloody hell."

I turned right when a gap appeared in the flow of traffic, and continued to turn right and right again, around the hotel complex until Mike got his bearings and began to successfully navigate us out of the city.

"The problem is they seemed to have changed the road numbering. All these maps contradict one another," he explained.

"I think the problem is that half the time you seem to be looking at the camera!" I snapped glancing across at him.

"That's because when I tried to print off a map for the centre of Nice my printer stopped working. So in a moment of genius…"

"You wore yourself out?"

"No! As I was saying, in a moment of genius I took a photograph of the monitor and I'm now using the photo of the map on the monitor to navigate."

It was indeed a good idea, just a shame the camera showed such a tiny image. Mike had zoomed in on the image and was constantly having to manipulate the picture in order to see where we were supposed to be going.

We joined a queue of traffic heading west, crossing a long, wide bridge over the river. The bridge carried not just several lanes of traffic but the railway as well and the parapets were lined with large urns. Once over the river the busy road ran between tall apartment buildings, with grander houses set back from the road, rows of shops and various office complexes. To the left the Mediterranean could be glimpsed, distant flashes of blue between the buildings. Palm trees grew in the central reservation, and from balconies luxuriant pot plants draped their leafy branches down the outside walls. It was a contrast from the cold, damp north of England where all the plants were rapidly losing their leaves and dying back for winter. Pedestrians walked briskly along the pavements, all the women looked chic and well groomed and many had pedigree dogs trotting alongside them on leads.

Soon the speed picked up and I needed to change gear. I've driven cars abroad on numerous occasions but there is always that initial period of adjustment to driving on the right, changing gear with the right hand, applying the handbrake with the right hand, judging distances from the kerb and so on. I was doing okay with the driving on the right bit and thought the gear changing was going okay too, until that is, a momentary lapse of concentration had my left hand reaching out to change gear, snagging the door handle instead and opening the door into a line of oncoming traffic.

"Argh!" I squealed, frantically slamming the door shut.

"What? What happened?" asked Mike, looking up from his map reading.

"Nothing dear, just getting a bit of air in, bit stuffy in here, not accustomed to all this nice weather," I babbled.

We left Nice heading towards Grasse and quickly found ourselves climbing away from the coast and up into the mountains. The region of Provence sits in the southeast corner of France, tucked between the Italian border to the east and the river Rhone to the west, the Mediterranean Sea to the south and to the north the regions of Ardeche, Drome and the Hautes-Alpes.

Provence-Cote d'Azur, to give the region its proper title, is divided into five departments covering an area of over eighteen and a half thousand square miles. With a population of just under five million, most of which are concentrated in the larger cities of Nice and Marseille, it is mainly peaceful and uncrowded.

In the eastern part of Provence the land rises steadily from the coast and as we drove inland that day we quickly gained altitude passing the Maritime Alps and then towards the mountains of Haute Provence. The flat, narrow plain by the coast was quickly left behind as we began a drive along switch-back roads, through wooded hillsides and small scatterings of towns and villages. Our ultimate destination was the village of Moustiers Sainte-Marie in the Verdon Gorge area of Provence, high in the hills and close to the Southern Alps.

Provence has long been a destination for foreign holiday makers and Brits seeking sunnier climes for their retirements, and looking back through history it seems that this is just one more wave of immigrants. Provence appears to be everything that is quintessentially French: sunshine, boules, the chic of the French Riviera, quiet countryside and architecturally stunning towns. But Provence has a chequered history and Nice, founded by the Greeks at the time us Brits were still collecting berries and chasing wild animals around, was for a time an independent republic, and Provence itself did not become a part of France until 1486. Prehistoric man left his mark in the form of rock carvings in caves in

Monaco which are thought to date back to a staggering one million B.C. Fast forward to a mere 60,000 B.C. and Neanderthal man hunted on the Riviera (it's possible a few are still there).

By 600 B.C. things were starting to get crowded: the Greeks arrived bringing the vine with them, those great traders the Phoenicians also came, quickly followed by the invading Celts. Hannibal passed through with his elephants on his way to the Alps. And then the Romans came, founding the region of Provincia. The Romans stayed for 600 years, a bit longer than they stayed in Britain, possibly due to the better climate, well you can't blame them. Their legacy can be seen around Provence in various towns and villages, from pottery, to bridges that are still standing, to aqueducts such as the magnificent three tier Pont du Gard near Nimes, the remains of temples, amphitheatres, the Roman arena at Arles and the Triumphal Arch at Orange. Whether it was the climate that helped all these structures to be preserved or not, one thing is certain, it highlights the Roman remains in Britain for the crumbling ruins they sadly are.

With the fall of the Roman Empire in the west, Provence saw wave after wave of invasion from less than friendly tribes: the Vandals, the Visigoths, the Franks to name but a few. Then the Saracens attacked, and then the Hungarians took their turn. We thought we had it bad in Britain what with the Vikings and Saxons but really the poor folk in Provence seem to have had non-stop trouble. By the early Middle Ages the Holy Roman Empire had got involved and from then on it seemed to be one thing after another. One result of all the troubles and civil wars was the characteristic fortified hill top villages of Provence which now seem so charming but at the time they were built must have been a refuge during terrifying times. And just as the twentieth century arrived and things looked like they were beginning to settle down the Nazis invaded.

We would be travelling through several larger towns before reaching our rented apartment in Moustiers Sainte-Marie, a small village where facilities would be limited and so we planned to stop off en route at a larger town to buy groceries for the week. Nice of course would have had plenty of supermarkets but in such a large place the difficulty would be finding them and so we didn't even attempt it. Instead when I saw an advertising hoarding for a supermarket located in Grasse I suggested we try to find it.

Needless to say we didn't find it but we did see quite a bit of Grasse as we drove aimlessly around. Like many of the towns in the region, Grasse is a mixture of old and new, although one of our guidebooks dismissed it as 'not one of Provence's most attractive towns'. Tumbling down the hillside the town is riddled with winding streets and tall buildings which I did find attractive. Grasse dubs itself as the perfume capital of the world, and was one of the locations used in the book and film 'Perfume'. Nowadays the town is famous for its sweet smell but this was not always the case. Back in the twelfth century Grasse had a large tanning industry which must have made the place stink! From the tanning of leather, industry developed into the manufacture of leather gloves and handbags and finally, thanks to a tanner and entrepreneur by the name of Galimard, into the perfume industry. He had the bright idea of making scented gloves and soon found a ready buyer for his gloves in the form of Catherine de Medici. She was so impressed she was soon bragging to all her wealthy friends and the industry took off. In the seventeenth and eighteenth centuries the perfume industry in Grasse began to develop as a separate industry from tanning, and at that time the plants used were grown in the surrounding countryside, today most of the plants are imported. By the nineteenth century Grasse had become popular as a place to holiday, Queen Victoria often spent the winter here, possibly to keep the heating bills for Windsor Castle down. The Galimard Company still exists along with around sixty perfume companies in Grasse and many of the larger factories offer tours. I don't really do perfume, I much prefer the smell of flowers in their natural state, and so having failed to find the supermarket we headed out of town.

Finding the road out of town was proving to be no easier than finding the supermarket. Road signs suddenly ceased to exist and it was a lucky guess on Mike's part that saw us heading up a steep, winding hill that climbed above the town.

"Are you sure this is the right way?" I asked with every hairpin bend in the road.

"Er… not really… yes… no… hang on… no, carry on…"

At the top of the hill the road straightened and we were rewarded with a sign confirming we were indeed going the right way. This was the Route Napoléon running from Grasse to Grenoble, and if we followed it all the way we would end up in the wrong place. So we weren't going to do that. What we did do was turn off it into a picnic site overlooking Grasse and the rolling hills descending to the plain and the Mediterranean in the distance. We stopped for lunch: sandwiches and chocolate brought from home in our rucksacks and a bottle of water from our suitcase that had survived the delicate ministrations of the baggage handlers. Initially Mike had suggested we could get a drink at a supermarket but I had ignored him, knowing his history when it comes to food shopping abroad, I had taken the precaution of bringing everything we needed for lunch. That first day, sitting in the open air in T-shirt and jeans, enjoying a picnic outside in October was a bit of a novelty, and certainly not something we would be doing if we'd been back in Britain. Wrapped up to the eyeballs in coats and hats and scarves, sheltering from the rain more likely!

An information board in the picnic site gave a little more detail about Route Napoléon and a useful map illustrated the road we would be taking that afternoon. Route Napoléon is, unsurprisingly, named after Napoléon Bonaparte and was opened in 1932. It follows the route taken by Napoléon in 1815 when he

21

left exile on Elbe to overthrow King Louis XVIII. Having abdicated the previous year Napoléon had soon changed his mind and set off to retake France. Whether his decision had anything to do with Louis reneging on his part of the deal and stopping paying Napoléon's pension is up for debate. But you would be cross if your two million Franc pension suddenly stopped, wouldn't you? And the media talk about public sector gold plated pensions! The Sun would have had a field day with old Napoléon's pension. I wonder if he stopped for lunch at the same picnic site? Possibly not, on arriving in Grasse the towns' people shut themselves in their houses, refusing to have anything to do with him, and so he and his troops struggled on across the mountains. He did succeed though, retaking the Royalist town of Sisteron and subsequently going on to rule France once more. But his success was not to last, he met his Waterloo at Waterloo later that year, leading the French to a defeat at the hands of the Duke of Wellington and the British army. And that probably lost him his pension for good!

Tuna mayonnaise sandwiches, chocolate and bottled water consumed, and our own pensions still some years away, we got back in the car and headed up the road towards Castellane, and hopefully a supermarket.

"Stop worrying, there's bound to be a supermarket at Castellane," said Mike.

I hoped he was right because it was the last place of any size we would be passing through. I was reminded of a holiday in Norway, where, getting low on bread and milk he had assured me there would be a shop at our next night's campsite. There wasn't and we drove miles out of the way looking for one without success. I swore then never to take any notice of him when it comes to shopping. Like Napoléon and his army I marched on my stomach, if I didn't have sufficient food I started getting anxious. And if the chocolate ran out, well!

At a little after two in the afternoon a winding road bordered closely by trees took us down into Castellane. This small town is one of the main resorts of the Verdon Gorge region and home to various companies providing guided activities such as canyoning, white water rafting and canoeing in the river gorge. Numerous signs pointed the way to a variety of campsites, now all closed for the season but in summer the place must be crowded with tourists. As we reached the outskirts of the town we crossed a wide bridge over the flowing river Verdon, above, on our right, perched atop a sheer limestone crag was the chapel of Notre-Dame-du-Roc. A winding path leads up to the chapel, passing the remains of the old ramparts, relics from a more turbulent past. The chapel may only date from the eighteenth century but there has been a shrine on the site, commemorating a holy miracle attributed to the Virgin Mary, which has been a place of pilgrimage for centuries.

As with so many towns in the region there has been a settlement at Castellane since before Roman times. The town has seen religious wars, Saracen invasions and the building of a large relatively new supermarket, which we found, much to my relief, on the far side of the town. The supermarket was closed, much to our chagrin. In fact, everything was closed. The whole of France closes for lunch – a fact we had forgotten about. Tills are emptied, blinds drawn, shutters closed and doors locked at midday and don't open again until, well whenever they feel like it, or so it seems. In the heat of a summer afternoon it made sense, but for us Brits who rarely experience the heat of a summer afternoon (unless you've got the heating on or put too much lighter fuel on the barbeque) it was an inconvenience that took some getting used to. With twenty four hour opening of supermarkets at home, corner shops and petrol stations selling milk, bread and other essentials from early in the morning until late at night every day of the year, we have become accustomed to being able to shop whenever we want. It's actually a rather nice idea that the shops do shut for lunch, it proves some things are regarded more highly than relentless commercialism. But it does take some getting used to!

"It's closed," I said as we drove into the car park.

"It can't be, it's a supermarket!"

"Well, we can stretch our legs and have a look round the town while we wait for it to open."

So, taking note of when the supermarket intended to open, we drove back through the town, parking in an almost empty car park overlooking the river and spent a pleasant half hour walking around Castellane, taking photographs of the narrow streets, the rushing river and the beautiful sycamore-lined square. Everything seemed to have a somnambulant air about it, it was rather nice this midday closing, although it did result in the town having the appearance of abandonment. Apart from a couple of tourists sitting at a pavement café we were the only people around.

We drove back to the supermarket through a town that seemed to be waking up, shutters were being thrown open, doors unlocked and people emerging from the houses like rats from Hamelin. The supermarket car park was full of cars and we found a space and set off to have some retail therapy.

"I'm really thirsty," commented Mike. "I suggest we buy a bottle of juice to drink now."

"Me too, good idea," I replied, scuffling about for some loose change and some carrier bags in my rucksack.

One thing about French supermarkets – and indeed Swiss, Norwegian and German ones too, not to mention Welsh ones – they do not give away carrier bags. I hate carrier bags, the waste, the pollution, the environmental cost, don't get me started! And so I always take reusable bags when I go shopping, and for once I had had the foresight to bring some with me on holiday. The previous year in the French Pyrenees I had forgotten and was standing at a checkout berating myself when I suddenly spotted some cardboard boxes tucked under the conveyor belt. Thinking they were like the ones supermarkets in Britain put out for customers to use I grabbed one and passed it to Mike who was standing at the end of the till ready to pack the shopping into his rucksack. But the cashier intercepted the box, said something neither of us understood and scanned a bar code on the box. It was at that point I realised I had just paid €1.50 for a cardboard box. Needless to say we got our money's worth out of it, taking it on every subsequent trip to a shop, I even tried to fit it in the suitcase at the end of the holiday, although Mike had something to say about that and so I had to leave my beloved, not to mention expensive, box behind.

So at Castellane I had come prepared. Although, it has to be said, not for everything. I realised as we entered the supermarket that I had forgotten to pack any shower gel or conditioner. Not a problem we were in a supermarket! We spent ten minutes scanning the aisles trying to differentiate washing up liquid and drain cleaner from shower gel and shampoo. My intention was to buy enough shopping to last the week, Mike though kept insisting we would be 'going past another shop later in the week'. Remember Norway, I kept reminding myself. So I ignored him until, that was, we came to the biscuits.

"I wonder if they have any of those chocolate sandwich biscuits we had in the Pyrenees?" Mike muttered.

"These?" I asked, pointing to entire shelf full.

"Brilliant! Grab a couple of packs."

"Why don't we get the special four pack?" I asked.

"Four! We'll never get through four packets of biscuits," he exclaimed.

I thought we would but for some reason I forgot I was ignoring him. Needless to say we ran out of biscuits on day three!

Forty stressful minutes later we left the supermarket with a trolley load of groceries that included some nice looking smoked sausages, several kilos of grapes, clementines and apples, crusty baguettes, smelly cheese, milk, conditioner, toilet paper and a mere two packets of biscuits. The toilet paper was a gamble that paid off. In England if you rent a holiday cottage it usually comes with bedding, towels and sufficient quantities of toilet paper. I had had the foresight to email the owner of the apartment we were staying in to see if linen was included – it was not, so we had brought our own. But with my abysmal French and a certain English reticence for all things lavatorial I had not felt able to ask about the toilet paper situation.

Our camping trip to the Pyrenees in July the previous year had rudely brought home to us the fact that French campsites do not provide toilet paper. Arriving late in the evening, having already called at a supermarket for supplies, we had pitched our tent and then gone down to the showers and toilets. An increasingly frantic search of every toilet cubicle had soon revealed there was not a scrap of paper to be found. I had sent Mike into the gents where, much to my relief (in more ways than one) he had found the arse end of a roll someone had left behind. (No puns intended, honestly). The next day the tiny village shop was closed. What can I say? It was France, it was a Sunday. So we had resorted to stealing toilet paper from the public toilets.

Fifteen months later and at the other side of the country, I was determined I would not spend another holiday squirreling away toilet paper whenever I passed a public toilet. Therefore I had made sure to purchase a six pack of loo roll.

"I don't think we'll need six rolls," Mike said as he loaded the shopping into the tiny back seat of the car, having failed to get it in the even tinier boot where the suitcase only just fit.

"You said that about the biscuits," I remarked, already regretting my decision not to buy more. "And mind that baguette! I don't want it breaking. Belt it in."

"I'll belt you in," muttered Mike as he carefully placed his two bottles of French beer into the foot well, before carelessly wedging the baguette behind the head restraints on the parcel shelf.

"If I have to do an emergency stop…"

"With your driving it's not inconceivable," he interrupted.

"Le baguette," I continued, determined to ignore him, "could come flying through the car and kill us both. And then, you wouldn't get to enjoy your beer. Although any more comments like that last one and you won't anyway!"

We were up in the high country now, a few thousand feet above sea level and the road out of Castellane followed the Verdon River as it began its passage between progressively higher river banks before reaching the spectacular Verdon Gorge. The gorge lies within the boundaries of the National Regional Park of Verdon. Formed to protect the area in 1997, the park covers 180,000 hectares. It was only forty six kilometres to Moustiers Sainte-Marie but the nature of the narrow road with its many curves and sharp bends made for a long if scenic route. Concentrating on not just driving on the right, but making allowances for doing so particularly with regard to the width of the car, was making for a tiring journey for me. The scenery was fabulous but it was little compensation as I dare hardly take my eyes off the winding road to admire the towering mountains, the narrow gorges, the aqua blue waters of the river and the colourful palette of autumn foliage.

At Point Sublime we pulled into the car park and walked the short distance out to the view point, staring down in awe at the river running into the deep sided Grand Canyon du Verdon some six hundred feet below. In one direction we could see straight into the canyon, the white limestone cliffs rising sheer from the river in some places. The colour of the river was stunning, a grey green attributed to the microscopic algae and minerals that it contains. It is thought that the name Verdon derives from the Latin word viridium meaning green. Trees in the bottom of the canyon added a contrasting splash of autumn colours, whilst many were still green some had begun to change to yellows, oranges and reds; as the week progressed we could see on an almost daily basis the green leaves giving way to the more colourful shades of autumn.

From Point Sublime we climbed again, the road turning away from the gorge before passing La Palud sur Verdon, little more than a small village hugging the road but in summer one of the main centres for tourists. Soon we were back with the gorge, at times hidden by the trees, at others close to the road with a sheer drop in places. The French didn't seem to be big on crash barriers. In the summer months, with the road busy with rental cars, caravans and campervans it would be a nightmare to drive, a constant stop start of inching along, giving way to oncoming larger vehicles and waiting for campervans to squeeze past one another. Another excellent reason why coming in spring or autumn was a good idea. Warning signs regularly appeared, some cautioning against falling rocks, others against ice. If the falling rocks from the hillsides and cliffs to the right didn't do you in, one patch of ice might have you plummeting over the edge and into the gorge on the left. Hopefully it would not be cold enough whilst we were on holiday to encounter any icy. The falling rocks though could happen at any time of year, and on several mornings that holiday we passed snow ploughs being utilised to clear rocks from the carriageway.

It had been a long drive when we finally reached a roundabout and a sign pointing right to Moustiers just three kilometres away. We arrived in the village at five in the afternoon and found our way to the car park by the cemetery. Parking the car, we climbed out and, as arranged, telephoned the owner of the apartment we were renting. We were both feeling a certain amount of anxiety at this point; until we were settled in the apartment there was still the unknown of what it would be like. Would we be able to communicate with the owner? Would we have to wait ages for her to meet us? Would she even answer the telephone? I dialled the number she had emailed to us but it didn't even connect. Tired, dehydrated, with the beginnings of a pounding headache, with not enough biscuits and a by now broken baguette, we both just wanted to sit down and have a cup of tea.

"It's not working," I said, glancing at Mike.

"Did you put the international code in?"

"No, because I just got some message saying 'welcome to France', when I turned the phone on," I explained.

"Try putting the international code in," he suggested.

"Okay." I did but it still did not connect the call.

"Did you put the zero in?"

"You're not supposed to put the zero in if you put the international code in!"

"Well try it anyway!"

I tried it and bingo! The phone started ringing.

"What's happening? Is it ringing?"

"Shh!"

There was a buzz and a click and the phone went to voicemail. I left a message in my best enunciated English.

"Voicemail?" asked Mike.

"Wee," I replied.

"There's a loo over there," he pointed further along the car park.

"What are you telling me that for? I've so little liquid in my system I probably won't need a wee until Tuesday!"

"Oh, you meant oui!"

"That's what I said! Anyway, what are we going to do now? Wait, I suppose."

"There's another number for her on this email." Mike read off a landline number and I tapped it into my mobile. It failed to connect.

"Did you put the international code in?"

"No, because my mobile knows it's in France!"

"Did you put the zero in?"

We tried every combination of international codes and zeros or lack thereof until after about four attempts the call was connected. We were both beginning to unravel by this time.

"Bonjour," came a tinny response from the mobile.

"Ah, yes, guten Tag," I gasped. Mike rolled his eyes. "I mean hello, er, bonjour,"

"Is that Julia?" asked Madame in perfect English.

"Ja, er yes, oui. We arrivez dans le er, cemetery." Mike did a bit more eye rolling.

"Bonn, okay I shall drive my husband's car and meet you there in ten minutes. Good bye."

"Sehr bonn, bonsoir," I replied disconnecting the call, and turning to see Mike shaking his head. "What's the matter with you?"

"You've spoken German, bad English and even worse French," he said with a chuckle.

"I think it's important to try. I would appreciate someone trying to speak English even if they couldn't. So I'm trying."

"You certainly are!"

We paced about by the car, anxiously scrutinising every vehicle that drove into the car park until eventually a white car drove up with a smiling lady looking out of the open window. She parked nearby and came over to greet us. Her English was almost as good as mine, although Mike later disputed that, saying she had near-perfect English.

Driving into the narrow cobbled streets and alleys of Moustiers Sainte-Marie is perhaps best left to locals, in any case parking spaces are virtually non-existent and so visitors and nearly all the locals park either in the series of small car parks close to the cemetery or on access roads below the village. So, leaving our cars and most of the shopping in the car park, Madame led us down the short lane into the village stopping to greet various locals she knew with much kissing of cheeks and rapid chatter. We followed her over a narrow bridge that crossed a rushing stream and pulled up short at a little door huddled between two shops. The door opened directly onto a flight of narrow stairs that were illuminated by a single energy saving bulb. A bulb that, as we were to discover, only became bright enough to assist you several minutes after you either stumbled up or fell down the stairs. She ushered us ahead of her up these treacherous stairs, I reached a landing and could just discern the vague outline of a door on the left and reached out gratefully for the handle but it was locked.

"No, no, to your right," instructed Madame.

I felt my way to the right, into an alcove with another door, also locked. I could hear Mike puffing and panting and banging the suitcase up the stairs behind me. Madame squeezed past to unlock the door and suddenly the tiny stairwell was flooded with light as she showed us into our apartment.

"So, zees is your apartment. I hope you like eet," she said, waving her arms to encompass the open plan kitchen and living room. Mike staggered in with the suitcase, nearly knocking the television flying before we had even handed over the €200 security deposit.

We had a guided tour of the apartment and a quick crash course on using the dishwasher, the gas hob and the thankfully still intact TV. With the deposit money handed over along with the money for the rental itself, Madame then began to give us a brief rundown of the shops in the village.

"Zere is zee bakery for your bread," she waved a hand in one direction. "Also down zees street ahead of us, zere is zee, er…. How do you say? I forget zee word… Er, zee shop for zee buying of er, moooo!"

"Meat!" I exclaimed.

"Oui, yes meat. What is zee word?"

"Butcher," I supplied.

"I am sorry, my English is not so good," she apologised.

"No, it is excellent," we both assured her.

Wishing us a pleasant stay and arranging to return the deposit on our last evening (providing the television and everything else was intact) she left us to unpack. Mike lugged the suitcase upstairs to the bedroom and I put the kettle on, shouting up to ask him to get the tea bags out of the suitcase. Now, I know, you can buy tea bags in France, but they are generally much more expensive and not from Yorkshire, so when going abroad I usually take teabags. This time I had got a bit carried away and taken enough tea bags to last for a month!

"How many cups of tea are you planning on drinking?" asked Mike, coming downstairs with a large bag of teabags. The irony that I had put them in a bag that had originally contained croissants from a supermarket back home was not lost on me.

"Well, about five in the next hour," I laughed. "Just one problem though."

"Oh, no what?" groaned Mike.

"If we want milk in our tea we are going to have to go and get the shopping! It's still in the car."

We grabbed the car keys and groped our way back down the gloomy stairwell, emerging into the evening twilight of the village street. It was a walk of just a couple of minutes back to the car from which we collected the carrier bags, the bottles of beer and the rather bent baguette.

"I told you to belt it in!"

We strolled back down the lane to the apartment, climbed the dark stairs once more, fumbled about trying to locate the key in the lock and finally got back into the apartment, beer and shopping intact but with a second bend in the baguette.

"You can't blame me for that," remarked Mike, heading for the kettle.

"No, I think she needs to put another glow worm in the jar."

We left the unpacking for the time being, and sat drinking tea and munching biscuits. A clock on the wall ticked away the minutes as we began to relax and rehydrate.

"It's nearly seven o'clock," gasped Mike, glancing at the clock.

"It's not," I replied as I checked my watch. "It's just gone half five. The clock's wrong."

We watched the clock as the second hand skidded down towards 6 and then struggled up towards 12. By the time it reached 10 it was labouring, two clicks for every second gained. At 12 it picked up again, rushing to 6 with the help of gravity, then labouring back up hill.

"Is it going to get to 10?" asked Mike.

"No, it's struggling with 8 this time."

We watched for another two minutes, barely able to take our eyes off it to pour another cup of tea from the dinky little pot. The level of tea in our cups and biscuits in the packet gradually went down as we sat riveted watching the travails of the second hand.

"Bet it can't get to 12 this time," said Mike.

"What the hell are we doing?" I exclaimed. "We've travelled goodness knows how many miles, spent goodness knows how much on airfare and car hire to escape the soggy British autumn, we're sitting in an apartment in Provence, surrounded by spectacular scenery and all we can do is watch a bloody second hand on a clock that needs a new battery!"

We ate another biscuit (I knew two packets would never be enough), drank the last of the tea and then went to unpack. After a shower and another pot of tea we set about preparing an evening meal. By mutual consent we had an easy meal of baguette, chorizo, cheese and fruit. The clock's second hand now seemed to be permanently stuck at 8 as we grabbed our coats and went out for an evening stroll through the quiet village. We were not out for more than an hour, the long day quickly caught up with us and an early night beckoned. Feeling more drained than the clock battery we were both asleep by 9.30.

€-€-€-€-€

By 10 p.m. we were both awake again. The village clock on the church tower was ringing out ten o'clock.

"I hope that doesn't ring every hour," Mike groaned sleepily.

It didn't ring every hour. It chimed the half hour too. But worse than that – it seemed to have a snooze facility! About five minutes after it chimed the hour it repeated itself, chiming the hour again just in case you missed it the first time, say if you were asleep or something! We fell asleep until 10.30. Then we fell asleep until 11 p.m. After which we got less than five minutes sleep before we were woken by the snooze chime. Twenty five minutes later and we were so knackered we actually slept through the half hour chime. But we certainly didn't manage to sleep through the midnight cacophony of 12 loud bongs, followed five minutes later with twelve more. Unlike Mike I quite like church bells, although by the end of the holiday I was having to re-evaluate that somewhat.

The next morning saw a rather sleepy Mike attempting to work the coffee machine. I don't like coffee so stuck to the easier to operate and fool proof combination of a kettle and a teapot and sat back to watch as Mike struggled and muttered his way towards a cup of coffee.

"Why they can't just stick to a nice simple cafetière I don't know," he moaned.

The coffee machine was a combined filter machine and a café-style barista machine. He couldn't make filter coffee as we didn't have any paper filters, and with all the instructions on the lid of the machine being in French he was struggling to figure out the intricacies of where to put the water in the barista part of the machine. I was on my second cup of tea and the second hand had progressed to 9 by the time Mike emitted a cry of triumph and coffee began to gurgle into his cup.

"Pass me the sugar please," he requested setting the small cup of coffee down on the breakfast bar.

I handed him a jar containing sugar lumps.

"Where did you get these from? I thought we bought a bag of sugar?"

"We did buy a bag of sugar, but this jar was already here."

"So we needn't have bothered spending all that time trying to find a packet of sugar in the supermarket yesterday?"

"Well if you put three lumps of sugar in every cup you make I think we'll need it!" I sighed.

"Three? Is that how many I put in?" he asked distractedly.

"Yes," I sighed.

The previous day we had struggled to find any white powdered sugar in the supermarket. There had been a gap on the shelf where it should have been and I had inadvertently picked up a bag of flour instead much to Mike's amusement. I had had the last laugh when he had spotted a single bag of sugar on the top shelf but had been unable to reach it, relying instead on my gangly arms to stretch up to get it.

Friday is market day in Moustiers and I was keen to get out, explore the village and sample the wares on the market stalls. As we left the apartment the village was just coming to life. The café opposite was just starting to make the first of a long supply of crepes

41

for passing tourists. The shops were opening and the locals were going about their daily lives, greeting one another, walking their dogs and carrying baguettes. It sounds like a cliché but it really isn't. Cats sat sunning themselves on walls and sparrows and magpies hopped along the pavements searching out crumbs between the cobbles.

Our apartment overlooked a small square where a fountain tumbled water into a trough and an olive tree provided shelter from the sun to customers at a pavement cafe. The square was surrounded by tall houses, most of which had shops or cafes on the ground floor and apartments upstairs. Moustiers is one of the main places to stay in the Verdon Gorge region, having approximately fifty apartments, twenty gites and over one hundred hotel rooms in the village, as well as nearly eight hundred camping spaces nearby. So it was likely that many of the apartments were rented out as was ours. In the height of summer I think we would have found the village too crowded with tourists, out of season it was perfect for us. Today tourism and the renowned pottery called faience which is made in the village are the mainstays of the economy. And even at the quieter time of year when we visited there were countless people who came at the weekend to browse the shops and admire and maybe even buy the ceramics.

Moustiers Ware or faience is tin-glazed earthenware. It was first made in the village in the fifteen hundreds when an Italian monk introduced the specialist technique. It took off, helped in part by Louis XIV who, finding the royal coffers a bit depleted, ordered all the gold and silver tableware to be melted down. With no gold plates to eat their baguettes, cheese and frogs' legs off ceramics moved in to fill the void; and the delicate, intricate white enamelled plates, jugs, bowls and soup tureens of Moustiers Ware soon became popular in many of the courts throughout Europe and not just in France. But of all the many things Britain excelled at during the nineteenth century one was pottery, and it was the likes of Wedgewood and Crown Derby, producing fine bone china and porcelain, that put an end to faience ware making in Moustiers. In the 1920s one man, the aptly named Marcel Provence, revived the tradition of faience making in Moustiers, and you could say it took off. Today there are over twenty workshops making these highly glazed ceramics, all decorated in their own distinctive style that range from delicate flowers, to beautifully detailed scenes, animals and mythical creatures. It is impossible to move in the village without encountering a shop selling these ceramics, some are quite large premises whilst are few are little more than grottos carved out of the rocks lining one of the approaches into the village. I took a liking to one delicately painted large jug, depicting a scene that incorporated Lowry-like figures in an autumnal woodland. However, when I saw the price tag I decided the price was not worth the cost should I drop it, chip it or ever risk using it. With my record for clumsiness I had best stick to Wilkinson's ware!

Whilst cleaning my mother's flat only the previous week I had had a mishap with an ornament. Well, actually it turned in to three mishaps. Dusting a shelf, I had flicked the duster over a carving of a deer standing under a signpost and the little wooden deer had dropped off its base. My mum had her back to me and was oblivious as I bent to pick the deer up off the rather loud patterned carpet, one of its hoofs had disappeared into the pattern and I was unable to find it (I did find it later but by then it was being sucked up into the vacuum cleaner). As I carefully set the deer back onto its tiny plinth, balancing it on three and a half legs, I continued dusting, picking up a carriage clock to give it a quick wipe. The back dropped off the clock as I lifted it up. Mum seemed not to hear the clatter and I hastily put the clock back together. Next on my dusting destruction derby was a small pottery donkey. Its leg fell off as I dusted it despite my by now overcautious cleaning technique. Mum was now tidying her kitchen as I quietly examined the donkey. I wasn't the first to break its leg, a patch of old dried glue marked the line of an earlier break. I put it back on the shelf next to the deer but the damage to the donkey was a little less easy to conceal, mainly because each time I tried to stand it up on the detached half of its leg the leg just fell over.

"The leg's dropped off your little donkey," I explained sheepishly as mum stopped tidying her kitchen and came to inspect my dusting.

"How has that happened? Were you being rough with it?" she asked, astute from many years' experience of my clumsiness.

"No, it's been broken and glued at some point in the past. Look you can see where the glue is!"

"Hm, it was probably you who broke it the first time!" she exclaimed, possibly correctly.

So, best not to risk buying any expensive pottery whilst we were on holiday! We crossed the square below our apartment, passing half a dozen small shops selling faience ware before reaching the parish church barely fifty yards away. The church, with its distinctive three storey Romanesque bell tower built using stones carved from fudge-coloured tufa, is a listed historic monument and dates back to the twelfth century. The doors were open so I went inside to look around, Mike followed, possibly with the intention of silencing the bells. From the Place de l' Eglise steps lead down into the church giving it an almost subterranean feel. High windows cast dim light down into the nave and onto the white marble altar, and it took a while for our eyes to adjust to the gloom. I had forgotten that although not officially a Catholic country, Catholicism was the main religion, and votive candles burned on a small side altar. A confessional made of carved old wood sat empty in one corner.

"It's a good job you're not religious," I whispered to Mike. "You'd be in there all morning."

"All morning? I'd be in there all year!" he muttered irreverently.

I'm not religious but I do like looking round old churches and graveyards. They give you such a flavour of history and provide a tangible link to the past and the people who lived then. The same feel can be gained from old houses but most people don't welcome you just walking into their home and having a good nosey about, and most old houses that are open to the public tend to be stately homes, and apart from a brief glimpse of life below stairs, they only really illustrate the lives of the privileged few.

The church might be twelfth century but people have been living here for over thirty thousand years, dwelling at first in caves. In the fifth century monks arrived and they too took a liking to the caves but after a hundred years they upgraded, building a monastery. The name Moustiers is derived from the word Monasterio. By the tenth century they had created a village on the site of the current village. Not long after and the Moors invaded and everyone rushed back to hide in the caves! In time things settled down again, the locals came back out of the caves, the fortifications were erected and mills were built which were powered by water from the streams. But Moustiers was not peaceful for long, the streams might provide power for the mills but they could also be destructive and twice the village was flooded, once in 1685 and again in 1702, destroying many of the houses.

Fortunately it was rebuilt and today Moustiers Sainte-Marie is officially listed as one of the prettiest villages in France. It is easy to see why. Narrow cobbled streets wind between tall houses with colourful shutters and red and orange tiled roofs. Stone doorways are often ornately carved and the wooden doors themselves all seem unique, with many being old, carved and studded with iron nails. Steeper streets and lanes are often stepped, and arches and alleys run between the rows of houses. There are numerous small squares and fountains, several with covered wash houses where once the women did the laundry whilst the men played chess, talked and smoked in the open squares. Over the many evening we stayed in Moustiers we explored the village, strolling the narrow lanes in the twilight and after dark, often finding ourselves at dead ends and even, on one occasion in someone's tiny garden. In the old village gardens are a rarity, the houses and lanes being so crammed in that there is barely room for patios or gardens.

In the lower part of the village, below the ramparts, the houses were less packed together, and here many properties had large gardens and vegetable plots. A stroll along the road marking the top of the rampart gave views down into gardens growing tomatoes, squashes, cabbages, sunflowers and potatoes. I have an apple tree and one year had a bumper crop of seven apples from it; these gardens had fig trees and one even had a peach tree heavy with fruit. I think I might be gardening in the wrong climate.

Dividing the village is a narrow gorge cut by the tumbling stream as it flows down a ravine that bisects the hillside. The cool damp gorge has created its own micro climate where lush ferns, mosses and other plants flourish in the shade. Just below the old village the remains of a narrow aqueduct that once provided water to the mills now carries water to gardens and allotments below. Springs and the stream feed the fountains which were once the only source of water for the villagers.

Moustiers seems to perch in a natural amphitheatre part way up the hillside and under sheer limestone cliffs that tower above the village and the valley below. Indeed many villages in Provence were built in this manner to protect the inhabitants and are known as perched villages. Sitting on a rocky ledge, that provides a natural line of defence, the village was further fortified with the building of ramparts and a wall running up the hillside around the town. Cut into the wall at the upper end of the village is an arched doorway, now open but once it would have been gated, and arrow slits in the wall above the gateway provide evidence of more troubled times in centuries past.

We walked down under an archway from the church, out into a wider road that runs above the ramparts and crosses the stream. This is the commercial centre of the village with a hotel, several restaurants, a bank, a grand war memorial listing the names of the men sacrificed during the Great War, yet more shops selling faience ware, the museum and the town hall. I was beginning to panic, thinking maybe the guide book was wrong, perhaps the market was only held in summer, but no, a little further along from the town hall and just before the police station, we came across the market.

There is something about a foreign market that seems more appealing than an English one; it must be the atmosphere because it is certainly not some of the very strongly smelling cheeses! There were not many stalls, one stall displayed an interesting range of bread of all shapes and sizes, two were selling fresh fruit and vegetables, a cheese stall was weighted down with massive rounds of cheese, smaller goats' cheeses, and slabs of butter. One stall sold nothing except dried herbs, the smell was intoxicating. The neighbouring stall sold solely mushrooms, fresh, dried and most exotic looking. Another stall had a large display of fresh fish, presumably brought up from the coast that morning, baskets of mussels and slabs of exotic looking wet fish sat next to a tray of spiny sea urchins that looked far too prickly and far too small to be worth eating. The middle aged man at the cheese stall offered me a sample of cheese which I politely declined. The rather sexy young man at the stall selling nothing but locally produced nougat offered me a sample of nougat which I politely accepted. No way was I going to decline that!

"What about me?" Mike asked me, watching as I salivated over the nougat and quite possibly the young nougat seller too.

"Get your own," I mumbled round a mouthful of deliciously chewy nougat.

The last stall on the row was not selling anything edible or even sea urchins. This particular stall was covered in a vast array of leather wallets, purses and handbags. I don't do handbags. If it won't fit in my pocket either I don't take it or I put it in a rucksack. But plenty of people do do handbags.

"Would you like me to buy you a nice handbag?" I asked Mike.

"No, I've nothing to go with it – you wouldn't buy me those Harris Tweed high heels in Lewis earlier this year."

Really there's no pleasing some people!

I would have quite liked to return to the nougat stall but I knew I would never be able to ask for a quarter of almond nougat and there was no way Mike was going to assist me. Instead we spent the rest of the morning exploring the village and the footpaths leading away from it before returning to the apartment for lunch.

The first of these paths took us past the cemetery and the small chapel next to it. The chapel came first (not sure what they did with their dead before then) but the chapel itself is sixteenth century. Dedicated to Sainte Anne, it was constructed using stones taken from the nearby village walls and the towers once dotted along it. Presumably by then the villagers had decided that the threat of invasion was less of a worry than the salvation of their souls. This up-cycling of old structures is nothing new and certainly not restricted to Provence or even France. In Britain there is plenty of evidence of old walls and buildings being plundered for their stone; many of the houses, farmsteads and field walls in the vicinity of Hadrian's Wall have been constructed using stone from the old Roman wall and the villas and forts along its length, and many of the old abbeys and monasteries that were destroyed at the time of the Reformation found their stones and timbers being used to build local secular buildings.

A twilight walk around the cemetery one evening later in the week proved a contrast between that and cemeteries at home. Because of the stony ground many burials had taken place in tombs, some of which were obviously family plots large enough to slide several coffins into. All the graves were immaculately tended and many depicted photographs of the deceased. A large number of graves bore Italian-sounding surnames, some possibly coming here in the early days of faience making, others no doubt immigrating during the nineteenth and twentieth centuries when Italians were escaping troubles at home and finding new homes all across Europe. Many Italians had settled in Britain, places like South Wales seeing a particularly high concentration of Italian immigrants. Some Italians even chose to put down roots in my home town of Burnley. Let me see: Burnley or Tenby or Provence?

Actually Burnley isn't leaping to mind as my first choice! As we wandered between the graves, coniferous needles and cones crunched underfoot, the yew and pines from which they had fallen providing shady spots between the graves. The cemetery was bounded by a high stone wall and heavy iron gates guarded the two entrances, security presumably to keep out the herd of wild goats that came down to the outskirts of the village after dark.

Beyond the chapel we followed a rocky path sign posted Sentier Botanique de Treguier. It followed the line of terraces heading south away from the village and remained quite level for some distance. Below us we passed another little car park and a boules pitch before passing olive groves containing ranks of ancient olive trees. The gnarled old trunks and twisted branches supported grey green leaves and the olives themselves were a mixture of young green fruit and ripening blacker fruit. I like olives, unlike Mike, so tried a nibble of a green olive. I wouldn't recommend it. The immature fruit was sour in the extreme and much to Mike's amusement I spat it out in disgust. Okay, I thought when I came to a black, ripe olive that I could reach, I'll try that. After a few seconds of chewing I spat that one out too, further amusing Mike. It was still sour although nowhere near as unpalatable as the first one, but an aftertaste of delicious olive oil did come through, enough for me to brave a few more black olives from other trees we passed.

Olives weren't the only things to tempt us along this botanical trail, where discrete information boards explained the various types of plants, trees and shrubs along the route. Mike was able to hazard a translation of most of the text and whilst some plants had their counterparts in Britain, some we did not recognise at all. Lavender, thyme and rosemary were obvious and I trailed along behind Mike sampling the herbs as we walked. The rosemary was particularly pungent, far stronger than the weedy shrub that struggles to survive in my damp Lancashire garden. Mike meanwhile was examining a plant that looked similar to a bilberry bush. Now bilberries have got to be my favourite wild fruit, nothing beats a bilberry crumble, except a bilberry crumble with clotted cream on top. In the north of England they are known as bilberries, but in other parts of the country they are called whinberries or whortleberries. The plant Mike was looking at had lost most of its leaves, although the shape and size of the bush was similar to a bilberry bush the fruit was darker and shinier and surviving much later in the year than at home.

"I think these are bilberries," he said, picking a fruit and popping it into his mouth.

"Hm, they look a bit similar," I said sceptically, wondering if our travel insurance covered us for plant poisoning. "What do they taste like?"

"Similar but slightly different," he replied.

"How do you feel?"

"Okay! Try one."

As he was still standing and shoving a few more into his mouth, I decided to take a chance. The initial flavour was not quite the same but then an aftertaste developed that did indeed taste remarkably like bilberries. Unfortunately there were no information boards relating to this particular shrub, so we never did find out if it was a relation of the bilberry. Still neither of us suffered any ill effects, and the fruit did taste delicious which was more than could be said for something we purchased at a supermarket later in the week.

The path continued, climbing gradually through woodland, leading us further round the hillside until views opened up of the valley and Lac de Sainte Croix, the azure body of water filling the valley. Green fields, grey green olive groves and, dotting the landscape, the tall, narrow dark green Cyprus trees seem to epitomise the landscape of Haute Provence. Birds called in the high branches of oak trees and crickets and grasshoppers chirped unseen in the under growth. Many of the leaves were changing colour from summer greens to yellows. One particular plant, similar to honeysuckle, displayed rich red leaves, whilst from another bush hung colourful red and yellow seed pods. This was one of several rather intriguing plants that lacked any information board to enlighten us. When opened the pods revealed not beans, as we had been expecting, but masses of fluffy seeds. Highly adapted to float on the wind and stick to anything they came into contact with, we were soon covered in fluffy seeds!

Above us we could hear climbers calling to one another as they dangled from ropes on the cliff face that rose behind the trees. The path continued to climb and we emerged from the wood onto a vantage point overlooking two canyons. Grasshoppers sunning themselves on the path leapt out of our way as we squeezed between thyme and rosemary plants and up onto the rocky pinnacle at the end of the footpath. The cool of the morning had been replaced by the warmth of the midday sun, jeans and jumpers now seemed superfluous, this was October and what a pleasant change from the weather at home. The silence was wonderful, a quiet peace undisturbed by traffic noise, just the occasional bird song or cricket call. After taking in the view and taking a few photographs we scrambled down from the pinnacle and retraced our route along the botanical trail back into the village.

€-€-€-€-€

A quick lunch of crusty baguette, ham and cheese, and a change of clothes from jeans and trainers to practical walking trousers and boots and we were back outside to take a different footpath through the village. A long queue had formed at the family run creperie just opposite our door as we crossed the square and took a narrow lane in the top left hand corner of the square that ran between shops and houses. The lane climbed out towards the ramparts and the fortified gateway, the Riou portal. A house, surrounded by a high stone wall, adjoining the gateway had a notice on the door: 'For Sale' and a mobile telephone number.

"I could live there," I said, gazing up towards the first floor of the house, all that was visible above the perimeter wall.

"No you couldn't," replied Mike, his usual response to any of my housing pipe dreams.

"I wonder how much it is…"

"Too much."

We passed through the gateway and the track lost any remaining tarmac, changing to a rough, stony path that contoured round the hillside. After a few yards, at the sharp bend in the track, an old stone bridge crossed a dried up stream. In wetter weather this would be the cascade that was marked on the map. The hillside rose up on the right at this point and below us, as we continued along the path, the views of Moustiers Sainte-Marie and the valley below opened up. Below the ramparts, houses and farms had sprung up as the village had grown in size and the risk of invasion had receded. Today numerous hotels, campsites, homes and restaurants occupy these lower slopes. We followed the path as it ran through an olive grove. I was full up after lunch so the olives were safe. We walked out between these characterful trees, with their gnarled curving branches, to reach the edge of one high terrace and stood admiring the view of the town and the panorama down the valley towards the lake. On the other side of the valley, wooded hills rose to a flat plateau.

The cooler morning had given way to a warm midday and temperatures continued to rise as the afternoon advanced. We found out later that we were lucky, this time of year was normally cooler and quite wet, we had picked an unseasonably dry week. It was possible to continue along the path, and either dip down towards the road leading back into the bottom of the village, or climb a higher path towards a hill called les Claux. We chose the higher route, but only ventured part of the way, choosing to stop at an old stone tower that seemed to be sitting abandoned amongst the higher olive groves. We sat for a while at a carved stone seat that had a small, carved stone table in front of it.

"I like this stone table and seat," I said wistfully.

"I knew you were going to say that!"

I'm afraid I have a habit of admiring things like seats, carved mantel pieces, items of garden furniture and then hinting madly that Mike might be able to recreate one for me. The poor man must be in a state of constant dread wondering what project I will spring on him next!

We retraced the track across the bridge, through the gateway and then turned off on a steep path, climbing a series of switch back steps that rose across the hillside revealing spectacular views of the roof tops of the village. A few families passed us, the children skipping down the path, making me jealous of their young knees.

At the top we reached the cobbled path leading through a stone gateway and up to the Chapel Notre-Dame de Beauvoir sitting perched on a rocky outcrop at the edge of a ravine. Just like the chapel by the cemetery, this chapel is also built on the site of an earlier one, in this case a Mariel temple built in the fifth century. The present chapel dates from around the twelfth century, although inevitably it has undergone some restoration since then.

A final flight of steps, flanked by tall cypress trees, carried us up to the open doors. Inside, the chapel with its high vaulted ceiling, was both darker and cooler in comparison to the warm sunshine outside. Candles flickered in ornate twin candelabra at the altar and light filtered in through the arched windows, picking out the ornate pillared altar with its intricate carvings and what appeared to be an immense amount of gold leaf decoration. The lower parts of the walls curving behind the altar were panelled in dark wood and the iron railing in front of the altar stood behind several stands holding scores of votive candles. At a table just inside the doorway more of these candles were available to buy. The more money you were prepared to spend, the bigger the candle and the longer the burn time. Did that mean if you could afford or chose to buy a bigger candle your prayer would go on for longer and have a better chance of being heard? That seemed a bit unfair to me! Maybe God paid more attention to the smaller, meeker ones.

Ever since the first chapel was erected back in the fifth century, the holy building has been a site of pilgrimage, just like the elevated chapel at Castellane. The faithful few still make the pilgrimage today, but mostly it is tourists who make their way up to the chapel. We made the pilgrimage ourselves several times during our stay, usually in the evening, after dark, to take atmospheric photographs of the chapel and the village below. The quickest route to the chapel from the village is following the cobbled path that climbs in a series of wide steps, passing twelve Stations of the Cross, all illuminated after dark. One guide book describes the path as an energetic walk of over 360 steps but according to the tourist information literature there are a more manageable 262 steps. Perhaps the author of the guide book slipped back down some of the steps and counted them twice. It was hard not to slip on the extremely smooth cobbles, presumably polished by the thousands of feet that had staggered up there and stumbled down over the years.

As we left the chapel the sun seemed stronger than ever. We retraced our steps a little way down and then passed through an arch in the wall to follow a narrow path that curved into the ravine. In winter and spring this ravine would be noisy with the sounds of the river cascading down from the mountain tops and through the village, but it, like the other cascade, was now dried up. We scrambled over boulders, worn smooth by water, and reached a more marked trail that carried us steeply up on the other side of the ravine. The gravel path was dusty underfoot and we climbed steeply, entering a line of coniferous trees before emerging onto the open hillside where the path levelled out. Now we had views across towards a further line of mountains in the east. A family picnicking nearby greeted us with cheery bonjours as we stopped for a drink and a breather.

Signposts pointed in various directions at a confluence of trails and we set off following the Chemin de la chaine which led round rocky outcrops, through low shrubs of juniper and rosemary until a final steep scramble brought us back to the edge of the ravine and the anchor point for the chain from which the trail takes its name. We crouched on the rocky edge and looked down, following with our eyes the line of a chain that stretched over two hundred metres across the ravine. Hanging from the middle of the chain is a five pointed gold leaf-covered star.

This star has only hung, like something recreating the Nativity, since 1957 but it is not the first to have twinkled over Moustiers. The earliest star to have been placed above the ravine dated to the thirteenth century and is thought to have been a bit smaller than the modern, man-sized one. Nor was it as heavy; the current star might be man-sized, measuring as it does 1.8 metres across, but it is certainly not man-sized when it comes to its weight (although I suppose it could depend on the man) the modern star apparently weighs in 150 kilograms. I just hoped the chain was as strong as it looked, you wouldn't want this star dropping on your head. Now in case you are wondering why the star was put there in the first place – after all it wouldn't have been easy back in the thirteenth century with no helicopters to lend a hand – you are not the only one! And of course as with many events from hundreds of years ago, there are various theories on the origin of the star.

So, the one the Tourist office goes with. Legend has it that in 1248 when King Louis IX (later St Louis) ruled France, he got it into his head that it was time someone had another go at driving the Muslims out of the Holy Land, and so he launched the Seventh Crusade. Never heard of the Seventh Crusade? No, me neither. First, second, third, yep. Richard the Lionheart and all that. Seventh? No. And as for Crusades four, five and six – well, what happened to them? You'd think that after six someone might start to realise that perhaps it might be a better idea to share the Holy Land. What am I saying? Eight centuries later and we still can't play nicely and share!

So, there's old Louis preparing to set off for the Middle East and soon to be canonised, possibly for knocking some Muslims about a bit (who knows?), could you imagine if we still did that today – Saint George W Bush, Saint Tony Blair – what a thought! Louis takes his army of knights and horses and footmen and all the paraphernalia of war and goes to do God's work of killing the Saracens. One of those knights was a Crusader from Moustiers Sainte-Marie, a chap named Blacas. Now Blacas didn't have much luck, although I dare say he had a sight better luck than some of his comrades and many of the Saracens. He was captured and imprisoned by them and he vowed that should he be released he would hang a star above his village and dedicate it to the Virgin Mary. And sure enough, in time he was freed and returned home to Moustiers where he fulfilled his vow. Nice story, happy ending (except for the Saracens) and a nice tourist attraction to boot. I hope that doesn't sound too cynical for it is not meant to be; the star really does add something to the village and the ravine, particularly as its origins date back to mediaeval times.

The star and the chapel tucked into the ravine are part of a celebration that takes place each year on 8th September. That day is the Day of the Nativity of the Virgin and is marked by the villagers, led by the village band playing pipes and beating drums, climbing up the hill to the chapel before returning to the square by the church for a traditional breakfast. The procession sets off quite early – 5 o'clock in the morning – another part of the tradition, or possibly because the church clock keeps everyone awake all night.

Having had a rest, a drink and a chance to take in the extensive views from the place where the chain is anchored into the rocks, we retraced our route to the junction of paths and turned right to follow the Chemin de Courchon. At first this route stayed relatively level before beginning to drop in a series of switch backs down towards the village. The path is a heavily built stone path, shored up with rock walls which give the impression of a Roman road or wall. In fact the path in its current form only dates back to the eighteenth century, nevertheless it is an impressive structure that must have taken considerable building. Back when it was constructed it was the main route from Castellane to the lower lying areas of Provence. Today it makes up one of many superb scenic footpaths in the area.

€-€-€-€-€

Mike was starting with a cold, snuffling, sneezing and blowing his nose and blaming the airline.

"Those budget airlines," he wheezed. "Just recirculating dirty air that's full of germs."

"I don't think that's exclusive to budget airlines," I commented as I put the kettle on for a cup of tea.

A sneeze was his only reply, followed by some noisy nose blowing.

"I'm okay, and I was on the same flight."

"If you mention man flu I shall…atchoo!"

"Gesundheit."

"That's German."

"I know that's German! I don't know 'bless you' in French."

"You don't know much in French," he mumbled, reaching for more toilet paper to blow his nose on.

The toilet paper was going down faster than the biscuits. It was fortunate that I had ignored him when he suggested we would not need a six pack of toilet paper for a week in Provence. At his current rate of usage we would need at least another pack. Oh well, we could get some when we went to buy more biscuits.

With Mike feeling sorry for himself and me less than keen to be seen walking through the village with a man carrying a roll of toilet paper, we decided to have an evening in. I curled up with a biscuit, a cup of Yorkshire's finest and a book. Mike read his map for a bit, but every time he sneezed the map was at risk of being either torn in two or covered in his budget airline germs.

"We could put the television on for a bit," I ventured as Mike sneezed, tutted and reached for yet more toilet paper.

"Oh that should be entertaining for you," he remarked.

The programmes, all three hundred channels-worth, were all in French. Okay, that was expected. Most seemed to consist of nothing but advertisements which made More Four and Channel Five back home look positively filled with something worth watching. After some squabbling over how to work the remote we eventually found a news channel. We still couldn't understand a word but at least we could guess at what was happening as the screen filled with footage and still photos of events. Some politicians were arguing. Italian air traffic controllers were striking – nice change from the French there. Barack Obama was talking but before we could tell what he was saying a voice-over in French drowned him out. And the seven thousandth crusade looked to be unravelling again in the Holy Land. We learned nothing new except that French news is as depressing as British news, even when you don't understand it.

Television turned off, biscuits eaten, second roll of toilet paper unwrapped, we went to bed.

"Good night."

"Good night. And don't breathe your germs on me!"

"No dear. Oh."

"Oh what?" I asked.

"I've just dropped the toilet roll on the floor and I can't see it in the dark."

Sighing, I sat up and fumbled about for the bedside light, finally finding it and switching it on. It didn't help. The apartment was very nice: clean, well equipped, comfortable, but the light in the bedroom, the only light in the bedroom, was an underpowered bulb (possibly a reject from a string of fairly lights or a twin of the one in the stairwell) and to make matters worse it was mounted in a cylindrical purple shade. A glow worm in a jar or Mike's red and shiny nose might have provided more illumination. Eventually Mike located the toilet roll, blew his nose and with the light turned out we went to sleep.

The church clock chiming the hour woke us up a little while later. Mike cursed, coughed, sneezed and bumbled about in the dark closing the windows. After that we slept much better, the bell was still audible but at least it was muffled. I say we slept much better but what I mean is Mike slept much better. I woke in the middle of the night, soaked in sweat and sticking to the sheets. I hoped I wasn't starting with a cold. I threw off the duvet but soon I was cold and was pulling it back on. This went on for the rest of the night. In the morning I had no sign of a cold. The same thing happened the following night: if we wanted a peaceful, bell-free night we had to close the windows. But then I started having hot flushes.

"It's your age!" stated Mike.

"I'm only forty-seven!"

"Menopause starting early," he exclaimed, nodding sagely.

"Well, divorce cured my P.M.T.," I teased. "Some women get violent mood swings, I believe, so I suggest you watch what you say!"

"Cup of tea my dear?" he wheedled.

Mike's cold disappeared after a day. The same could not be said for my hot flushes but I'm blaming the balmy Provence climate and not my age. For the rest of the holiday there was a nightly point of conflict as we debated (argued) whether to have a bedroom window open or closed during the night.

If the nights were too warm, for me at least, the day time temperatures were just right. Our first morning away from Moustiers started with a cool edge but soon warmed up. We followed the road back towards Castellane and Point Sublime, parking down a surprisingly wide side road that led into the canyon. This is the only road that actually comes close to the bottom of the Verdon Gorge and is a popular place to park for many walkers embarking on the Sentier Martel, the Martel Footpath, which explained its width. The road wiggled down through woodland towards the start of the Grand Canyon du Verdon, the upper reach of the Verdon Gorge proper.

The Verdon Gorge runs for 21 km, a steep cut limestone gorge that has been carved out over millennia by the eroding action of the Verdon River. In places the cliffs are sheer, stretching hundreds of metres from top to bottom, whilst on some stretches the gorge widens and the lower slopes are shallower before steepening to cliffs higher up. At its deepest the gorge is a colossal 700 metres or 2300 feet, making it the deepest in Europe. There is no complete footpath through the gorge but a series of paths on either side run for part of its length. The Sentier Martel is 14 km long and is generally graded by the guide books as strenuous, only seasoned walkers are advised to attempt it. Indeed, the warnings are enough to put people off and granted it's not the sort of Sunday afternoon stroll I would consider taking my elderly mother on, but that said, you don't need to be Chris Bonnington either.

The Verdon Gorge had never really been completely explored until the beginning of the twentieth century. But in 1905 the French Government decided to look into using the gorge and the Verdon River as a means of water supply. They sent in a geologist called Edouard Martel to survey the gorge. His expedition was the first to venture down the river, he took three days and his findings were good news for the Government. In 1928 the French Touring Club, which sounds like it ought to be something to do with cycling not walking, opened the first footpath, the Sentier Martel, named in honour of the geologist. Since then the path has undergone some improvement as we to discover for ourselves.

It is possible to walk the whole of the Sentier Martel, a trip estimated to take around six or seven hours, emerging back onto the road at Chalet de la Maline. We didn't do that for a very good reason: we would have been faced by a long walk back along the road to the starting point. In summer a shuttle bus runs between Point Sublime and the Chalet, for anyone walking in Verdon in July and August that is one option, the other would be to leave a car at each end. Obviously neither of these options was available to us. So we had decided to walk part way to La Mescala, a natural half way point as it was where the river bent sharply changing from flowing south to flowing west. The walk back would be equally enjoyable with views in the opposite direction.

We arrived quite early in the morning and were amongst the first to park. There was a cold nip in the air and we wrapped up against the early morning chill. In the narrow canyon the autumn sun was slow to reach to the bottom of the gorge, in some spots failing entirely, and it was mid-morning before we shed a layer and later another layer until by lunch time we were comfortably warm wearing just T-shirts.

Steps led down from the road, quickly carrying us close to the water where a large notice, one of several we were to see at many points on the start of trails near the river, warned that the river could rise suddenly. Paddling and bathing were not permitted. The river now feeds into a massive man-made lake further downstream, the end of this lake is dammed and used to create electricity at a hydroelectric power station. The sign was in about six languages and all bar one pretty much used the phrase hydroelectricity, even I could work that out! But that was far too straight forward for German, in that language the translation was something far more wordy! Well, it would be wouldn't it? Why use one word and a dozen letters when four words and most of the alphabet could be used instead?

Apart from the risk of being swept away there is an important ecological reason not to go into the water, disturbing the shingle. The Verdon River can boast one of the rarest fish in Europe, the apron fish, a trout-shaped grey stripy creature which breeds in very few places, the Verdon Gorge being one of them. It lays its eggs in shallow scrapes in the gravel and is very susceptible to disturbance. Information signs in various places asked walkers not to paddle and not to throw stones, and explained the importance of this rare fish. The information signs failed only to explain how the fish coped with the sudden increases in water level.

The water was flowing quite strongly in places as it tumbled over boulders and weaved its way along the undulating river banks. But in the dry autumn the river level was nevertheless relatively low, presumably it would be much higher in the spring and summer after winter snow melt and wet weather. It would need to be for the white water rafting to take place, otherwise the money paying public would find themselves doing more carrying than rafting.

From the warning notice it was a very brief walk close to the river before a short flight of metal steps carried us part way up the cliffs towards a tunnel. This was the first of three tunnels and the longest, stretching for over 600 metres. Mike got his head torch out of his rucksack and switched it on. The beam disappeared into blackness. We walked along in relative peace, the tumbling waters of the Verdon River dwindled to silence and only the drip of water and our feet splashing into occasional puddles sounded to disturb the eerie stillness. In a few places windows, guarded with sturdy metal gates, were cut into the side of the tunnel giving access to rock climbs down into the gorge. The light from these windows and the torches of people walking towards us were the only illumination to be seen.

On every walk people always said 'bonjour' as we passed. But suddenly this stopped when we entered the tunnel. It was almost as if, unable to see one another, no one was willing to call out a greeting in case they should be saying hello to an axe murder or someone equally unsavoury like Boris Johnson. It was very strange. Also strange was that no one made any sounds, no one chatted to their companions, no one tried to make echoes ring out, no one clapped their hands or whistled. It could have been a tunnel full of zombies walking past us. I could not imagine that happening in Britain, there is always someone, usually a dad, making odd gibbon noises or calling 'echo' to entertain his kids and embarrass his wife.

"Oooh!" Mike began to howl.

I knew what was coming – he was going to try to get some resonating echoes going!

"Ooooooh!"

"Shut up!" I whispered urgently. Just because no one could see us I wasn't prepared to have him embarrassing me.

We emerged from the first tunnel to the sound of rushing water and the glare of sunlight but soon we were plunged back into another, shorter, tunnel. At only 100 metres long, we were able to pick out the pin prick of light at the other end, and soon found ourselves emerging into daylight once more.

These tunnels, together with a third tunnel close by, had been created as a result of the surveys carried out by Monsieur Martel and the subsequent decisions of the French Government to create a hydroelectric scheme on the Verdon River. The scheme never came to fruition. The third tunnel is disused and the first two have been incorporated into the Sentier Martel, in fact without these tunnels the path would not be possible.

After the tunnels the path wound up and down along the gorge, at times bringing us close to the river and at other times climbing away from the water. Sun shone into the canyon, often leaving lower areas in shade. The rocky path kicked up white dust onto our boots, a nice change from the mud we would be kicking up back home at this time of year. Trees were taking on their autumn colours, pale yellows and russets of larger trees and vibrant reds of shrubs growing close to the path. To come in autumn must be to experience some of the best of the flora of the area. Jays chattered noisily in the trees, whilst the quieter piping call of great tits filtered down from many branches. Boxwood is a common plant of the region and great swathes of it filled some lower parts of the canyon. Something had been digging and scratching around the roots of many of the trees and shrubs, making the ground in some areas look like it had been dug over. We wondered what animal had made the scrapes and ruts, could it be wild boar? But we saw no mammals to account for the activity.

As we neared the bend in the river the sides of the gorge seemed to close in, the white cliffs towering up above our heads. In places we followed the path as it ran along narrow rocky ledges hewn out of the cliff, and I was grateful for the reassuring presence of a wire rope strung along the wall of the cliff to act as a hand rail. Just before reaching la Mescala the path ran out. The way was blocked by a wall of rock and a sheer narrow ravine running up it. The Touring Club had overcome this with a long flight of steep metal ladders fixed into the ravine. Apparently there are some two hundred and forty steps, I didn't count them, I was too busy making sure I didn't bark my shins on the narrow risers and too busy posing at various times to give perspective to Mike's numerous photographs. In a few places broader landings allowed walkers to pass where the ladders switched back on themselves. In other places it seemed you were scraping past the rock on both sides as the walls of the ravine seemed to close in further.

73

At the top we came out onto a narrow path, a quick scramble onto the top of a rock and we were treated to almost uninterrupted views up the canyon and down to the blue green water of the river far below. Jays flew past as we looked down onto tree tops of tangerine coloured beech leaves. A small bird flew below us, wings beating for a few seconds before staying open in a glide. Mainly grey in appearance, it had distinctive red patches on the wings which I tried to remember for later identification. The (much) later identification courtesy of a very good bird book Mike had bought me for Christmas the previous year, revealed the bird to be a wallcreeper, a relative of the nuthatch. These quite elusive birds are usually found between one and three thousand metres above sea level, and the lush woodlands, river and sheer cliffs of the Verdon Gorge suit it perfectly. As its name aptly implies, the wallcreeper creeps along the cliff faces, hunting out insects and building nests in the cliffs. From the description in the book, it was likely to have been a female bird that we saw, males have much more red on their wings.

We scrambled down the rock and re-joined the path, descending steeply for a short distance before we reached a junction. If we carried straight on the Sentier Marcel would eventually take us to Chalet de la Maline, but that path was for another day. Instead we took the left hand path that doubled back downhill, taking us through dense woodland where dappled shade cooled the sweat created by the long flight of steps. The sound of the river grew as we emerged onto a smooth rocky lip at the edge of a gravel beach and the sharp bend in the river. This was La Mescala, a name that I was no doubt mispronouncing every time I said it out loud. We teetered down the sharp gradient of the smooth rocks, jumping the last couple of feet to the shingle beach. The far bank was not far at all, just a few metres across the smoothly flowing water. To our right the river flowed quietly on and out of sight round a gentle curve, seeming to almost disappear into the rocky canyon. To the left, the river flowed out of the narrow canyon we had just traversed along, the very end of this section of the canyon was marked by a shallow limestone cliff at the water's edge, the layers in the rock clearly visible, atop this small cliff a stand of young oaks with yellowing leaves were growing. On the far outer side of the bend a small feeder canyon joined the main gorge. Anywhere else this, the Canyon de l'Artuby, would have been spectacular in its own right, but running into the massive Verdon Gorge, it became a little overshadow both in size and reputation. The Artuby River was almost dried up, little more than a trickle joined the main canyon, but in spring and summer it would be a fast flowing addition to the main river.

We took a few photos before sitting down on one of the low rock ledges above the shingle to eat lunch. A couple a little further round the bend than us, (metaphorically, that probably takes some doing) were just finishing their sandwiches and soon packed up and headed off. We were left alone with the solitude and the call of birds. But not for long. Children's voices could be heard drawing nearer

75

down the path and soon a small army of them appeared, jumping down onto the shingle, dashing along the beach, scrambling over the rocks and skimming pebbles across the smooth water. Their ages varied from a rather desultory girl in her mid-teens, who clearly thought all this scenic beauty was beneath her; an older boy who was going out of his way to win her affections (it wasn't going to happen, you could tell from her expression); a teenage lad clad all in camouflage combat gear, two boys aged about ten who competed noisily with their game of ducks and drakes, a girl of about seven who seemed to be as graceful as I had been at that, and most other, ages, adorned as she was with a streak of mud down her backside and on both knees; and bringing up the rear was a boy of about five years old who was chatting rapidly to himself and being ignored by everyone else. The two sets of parents appeared with heavily laden rucksacks a few minutes later, by which time the teenage girl had swapped her walking boots for some slip-on white pumps (damn! Why hadn't I thought to dress for dinner?) and the younger children had lined themselves up along the rock ledge on either side of us. I felt trapped. It was like being back at work. The peace had been obliterated and yes, they had every right to be there, but it really was bad timing!

We pushed our remaining bars of chocolate back into our rucksacks and set off back up the path. We could eat them a little later, a good excuse for another rest stop. Not that we needed a rest stop, despite signs and trail guides warning of the strenuousness and difficulty of the Sentier Martel, it was actually less arduous than most hill walks in the Lake District or the Yorkshire Dales. The steep flight of metal steps was now an easy descent although my knees were aching by the time I reached the bottom. The scenery was different on the way back, the sun had travelled round the gorge and was throwing sunlight onto different areas of the cliffs and woodland, creating different colours and photo opportunities. Scenery that had been over exposed by the morning sun was now cast in shadow, making photographer Mike a happy snapper. In other areas the sunlight caught the autumn colours of the foliage, bringing out the wonderful variations of pigment in the leaves of the different tree species.

More people were now on the trail, giving me plenty of opportunity to practice my French accent as I returned every 'bonjour'. Practice makes perfect, well sometimes. Just before we reached another series of steps cut into the rock leading down to the river we stopped. These steps carried us past a scree slope of rubble that had been dug out from the third tunnel, and Mike was keen to see this tunnel. Leaving his rucksack, he set off scrambling up the scree slope. I don't like scree slopes so I left him to his little adventure and soon found myself watching a pair of gold crests that were flitting between some boxwood shrubs. A few minutes later a cascade of pebbles and grit preceded Mike's return. Torch in hand he eagerly explained that much to his surprise the tunnel was open, although he had not ventured in.

Personally I prefer gold crests to abandoned tunnels; I guess I'm just strange that way.

We walked the remaining two tunnels, blasts of cool air coming out to greet us as we neared the entrances. In the morning they had seemed chilly but now we welcomed the cool darkness after the heat of mid-afternoon. Hordes of walkers were streaming through the tunnels, and we were glad of our decision to make an early start that day, at least we had had the path to ourselves for most of the morning. The road, when we climbed back up to it a little while later, was crowded with parked cars, and many people were walking down the path from the hillside from Point Sublime. That day was one of the busiest we experienced, no doubt because it was the weekend.

A drink and our remaining bar of chocolate seemed like a good idea and we sat a little above the road, on the edge of the path to Point Sublime, seated under a rocky overhang with views over the shrubs to the river and cliffs opposite. A blind path led off through an arch to a viewing point above another tributary of the Verdon, le Bau, a much smaller river that drained from a valley in the high hills above the villages of La Palud sur Verdon and Chateauneuf les Moustiers.

€-€-€-€-€

There was still plenty of daylight left and so we drove back to La Palud sur Verdon, turning right in the village and taking a progressively narrower road that wound first through woodland and then more open country before dividing into two. We took the left hand turn on an even smaller road that ran out some way short of the ruined village of Chateauneuf les Moustiers.

Parking at the start of a dusty track we set off towards the village. The sun beat down on the dusty fields bordered by wire fences and hedges. Under the shade of some trees we came across a small herd of goats, bells around their necks clanging melodically as they pulled at the sparse vegetation. Oak trees lining the track closer to the village had shed hundreds of brown acorns that crunched under foot as we walked up the track. The leaves of these green oaks had changed to autumn browns.

As the track ran out we reached the edge of the village. The reason there was only a track to the village instead of a metalled road was a sad tale, and a small white stone war memorial just below the ruined houses bore witness to the terrible effect of the Great War. Ten names were carved into the humble memorial; three of the ten shared the same surname. These ten names represented all the young men in the village at the time of the First World War. Their fate reflected the fate of their village. With no men to tend the flocks and harvest the crops, no husbands, sons or brothers returning to Chateauneuf, the village slowly died too. By the start of the Second World War there was no one left.

A settlement had existed on this site since the end of the eleventh century. Who, amongst those first settlers, alive in an age when war consisted of bows and arrows and trebuchets, could ever have imagined the mechanised warfare that would slaughter men in their millions and sound the death knell of their village almost a millennium into the future? At the time the village developed it was located on an old Roman road. Ownership of the village passed down the centuries through various noble families. A castle was built here in the fifteenth century and a church in the eighteenth. By the late nineteenth century the village had a thriving population of nearly six hundred. But the village began to decline following the building of a new road further down the hillside that bypassed Chateauneuf, going through La Palud sur Verdon instead.

We followed the marked trail through the village, passing ruins of the houses and cottages, and the old church. Lanes grown thick with grass ran between the crumbling house walls, the roofs tumbled in, thick old beams sagged and thick brambles and grasses grew where once families had lived. Lizards that had been sunning themselves caught our eye as they dashed over the stones, disturbed by our approach. Blackbirds and sparrows flew between the decaying walls, and wild flowers peeked between the stones. It was a sad sight. In the Spanish Pyrenees the previous summer we had visited abandoned villages there too; in these ghostly places all the residents had been driven out during the Spanish Civil War.

If you follow the line of the old Roman road away from the village, climbing a small rise and continuing towards the northwest, the valley opens up below you, ridges of mountains marching away towards the Alps. This ancient road hugs the side of the hill, running under steep rocky slopes on the left. A short walk along the track brought us to the sixteenth century Chapel Notre Dame de la Baume. This arched roof little chapel is almost hidden being built just inside the entrance to a shallow cave.

We returned to the hire car, walking down the track from the village, views across the fields of Haute Provence stretched in front of us, with the rocks of the canyon and the wooded slopes marking the river valley towards Castellane. The drive towards La Palud was unremarkable until we reached a narrower part where woodland closed in on either side. The side of the road on the right was marked by a bank of two or three feet with rocks sticking out between tree roots and soil. I was just about to voice the thought that I hoped we didn't encounter a car coming in the other direction when we encountered something worse.

Britain obviously doesn't have the international monopoly on the clichéd white van man, although the Ford Transit whizzing towards us was more minibus than van. I slammed the brakes on, pulling over to the side of the road but there was not much room. The minibus slowed too but then stopped, I inched forward but could go no further as a rock was protruding out of the bank.

"He won't get through there," remarked Mike, glancing across at the gap on our left. "Try going a bit further forward."

"I would if I could, but there's a rock, you won't be able to see it now but I'm nearly touching it."

Both of us were thinking about the insurance excess as Mike opened the window and stuck his head out to see just how close I was to the rock (close) but the driver of the van wasn't bothered about rocks, or trees for that matter! He suddenly lurched off the road, nearside wheels churning up soil and bouncing over tree roots, offside wheels squealing for grip on the tarmac as he forged a way past us.

"Don't go forward!" warned Mike unnecessarily as I put the gear lever into reverse and turned the wheel, easing away from the €700 insurance excess.

"Ici le boulder," I pointed as the jagged rock came into view beyond the front wing.

Mike rolled his eyes.

Safely back in Moustiers we settled down for a meal of smoked sausage casserole with crusty baguette, followed by tinned fruit and emulsion paint as Mike referred to the plain yoghurt I spooned onto the pears. The sausage casserole was delicious and we both agreed we should buy some more smoked sausage later in the week to make another one.

The next morning we were up extra early, the clocks had just gone back onto the French equivalent of our day light saving. Mike was worried with darkness coming at 6 p.m. we would not have enough daylight to fit in a full walk that day. So at 6 a.m. the alarm clock on my phone work us both up, within a millisecond the clock bells in the church were also chiming the hour. Five minutes later I was in the shower and the snooze facility on the church was waking Mike up again.

"Vite! Get up lazy," I called through to the bedroom. "You were the one insisting on an early start."

I came out of the bathroom to find Mike stumbling about in the dimly lit bedroom, trying to put a fleece jumper on.

"What's up with this?" he snapped.

"It's too small for you," I replied.

"I've not eaten that many baguettes!"

"It's too small for you because…"

"Is this your fleece?"

"Oui," I sighed. "Are my knickers safe or have you put them on as well?"

He had accidentally tried to put my jeans on once, well he says it was accidentally. After jumping about trying to pull them up over his thighs he had eventually snapped, "These are yours! How on earth do you get them over your bum?"

"Thanks!" I had replied, before he ruefully realised his commented had quite unintentionally sounded rather insulting.

"Sorry, my dear, I didn't mean it quite like that."

I had forgiven him but I certainly hadn't let him forget it.

With my clothes repatriated and Mike wearing his own, we went downstairs to a breakfast of baguette, butter, jam and cheese. A hastily made packed lunch consisting of more baguette and ham and lots of chocolate was thrown into the rucksacks and we set off into an early morning village where only the crepe man was stirring.

We were heading for the Sentier de l'Imbut on the southern side of the Verdon Gorge, driving down towards the lake and taking the bridge that crossed the river as it came out of the canyon. Soon we turned off the main road, taking a road signposted to the village of Aiguines, climbing the hill in a long series of switch backs. At first we were driving through oak woodland and suddenly a fox darted out of the trees some distance ahead of us and dashed across the road. A little further and the landscape opened up as fields bordered the road, they had recently been ploughed and the dry stony soil still lay in distinctive lines.

We climbed and climbed. At Aiguines, vineyards and a restored chateau contrasted with the quite modern design of a visitor centre. The main road through the village squeezed through a narrow gap between tall shuttered buildings before widening considerably into a sycamore lined square. Shops that advertised honey and lavender were still to open for the day. Lavender is a major crop of the flat plains and plateaux of Provence and the honey a by-product and we saw many roadside stalls selling lavender honey as we travelled about the region.

The road climbed above Aiguines and we stopped to admire the views of Lac de Sainte Croix, glistening bright blue in the distance. In the foreground just below us were the red tiled roofs of the village and the grounds of the chateau. Lines of vines grew below the restored seventeenth century chateau, and a simple church with bell tower and a small graveyard were located to the left of it. But it was the chateau itself that was the most eye-catching, sitting four square, with round turrets at each corner, and the cream walls reflecting the morning sun. The main roof of the chateau was covered with traditional red tiles, but the funnel shaped roofs of the turrets were each decorated with a different pattern of glazed coloured tiles.

Soon the road was running closer to the gorge, although views were mainly obscured by dense woodland where oak dominated. There are various species of oak that grow in the Verdon region, green and white oak being amongst them. Unlike at home not all of the oaks are deciduous and we saw many oaks that had quite waxy almost spikey leaves and very elongated pointed acorns.

Mike pointed out an information board as we drove past. "That's where the path comes out from the gorge."

"Do we have to walk back along the road?" I asked; it seemed a little bit of an anti-climax if we had to trudge along the tarmac at the end of the walk.

"No, there's a path nearby that goes up into the woods and then runs parallel to the road back to where we will be parking."

"Tres bien."

"Very good," Mike said, sounding impressed.

"Merci."

A little further on we reached a hotel, set back from the road and clinging to the top of the cliff above the gorge. On the opposite side of the road was a car park and I pulled in and parked. Our walk started a little way back along the road just beyond the hotel grounds. Sentier de l'Imbut is graded as even more strenuous than Sentier Martel, although having not found Martel strenuous I was not too worried about this footpath, until that is…

"This is the one I told you about," Mike said, interrupting my thoughts.

86

"What do you mean?"

"There are some quite narrow sections above the river with metal wires bolted into the rock face, and then there are the ladders, and the climb out is steep with some climbing."

Oh, now he told me! What if I got part way up and then couldn't get out? What if I froze? What if I couldn't go forward or back? He had tried to take me up an almost vertical rock face in the Ordesa Canyon in the Pyrenees and I had had to have an assertive word with him.

"And the route up and out is one way only because it's so steep and narrow," he added.

"That's not making me feel any better!"

"You did that via ferrata in Switzerland, you'll be fine."

"I was wearing a hard hat, a harness and several Tena Lady, and was clipped in to a fixed wire rope the whole time! Plus I was younger and dafter and didn't have a clue what I was letting myself in for!" I exclaimed as I remembered standing on a metal hoop fastened into a sheer cliff face with nothing but two thousand feet of thin air between me and the floor of the Lauterbrunnen valley.

"You'll be fine. You don't need a rope."

"Hmph!"

Believing me suitably reassured Mike led the way off
the road and into the shrubbery. If it sounds a bit
vague, that's because it was. A signpost pointed
along a path that disappeared between a couple of
bushes where it immediately petered out. Mike
forged ahead muttering something about pruning and
path maintenance, and I bravely followed him
muttering something about being out of my mind.

"Ah! This is it. This way," he exclaimed, as the path
once more reappeared.

We were dropping steeply, following a rather vague
path that wound between saplings thick with lichen
and growing so close together that little light
penetrated to the forest floor. Dead leaves and soil
compressed under our feet. The saplings thinned out
as we neared a rocky edge. Mike went first left and
then right, trying to find the route down. All
footpaths signs, usually yellow or white lines on trees
or rocks, were conspicuously absent. He tried
scrambling down to the left but soon scrambled back
up again; I waited, unwilling to commit until he knew
where we were supposed to be going. He tried
heading right along the edge of the rock and soon was
calling that he had found the path again, at which
point I followed him.

It was a steep but relatively easy climb down the
rocks and soon we were back in amongst the trees on
a by now obvious path that needed no marking, so of
course there was a yellow marker. It is often the way!
A zigzagging path carried us down to the river, nearly

eight hundred feet below the road and we turned left, heading downstream towards an arched wooden and metal bridge. This is the only crossing point of the Verdon River for its whole journey through the gorge. We would not be crossing the river, our footpath was all along the south bank, but we walked into the centre of the bridge to enjoy views up and downstream. As we stood watching the quietly flowing water beneath our feet another walker appeared from the other bank and began crossing the bridge towards us. He was carrying a huge rucksack with a camping roll fastened to the top which suggested he was walking one of the long distance GR routes in the area. GR stands for Grand Randonnee, the French equivalent of our National Trails. The only thing he seemed to lack was a map and he stopped to ask for directions. Mike showed him the map as they conversed in a mixture of French and English. I kept quiet and admired his muscular calves. The French walker thanked us and crossed the bridge, quickly disappearing into the trees.

We followed at a more leisurely pace and began walking along the dusty path as it wound between trees, keeping close to the river. The canyon was quite narrow at this point and very rocky, with few trees growing in the bottom. The path soon began climbing up the canyon walls, scaling the bottom of the rocky cliffs as they pushed out towards the river bank. There was no significant altitude gain, we remained for the most part within twenty or thirty feet of the bottom of the gorge but the path was now running along the edges of the cliff face and was only possible due to the wire ropes bolted into the rock face that gave not just something to hold onto but a reassuring feeling of safety. Mike was correct, I did not need the harness and hard hat, the path was fun and exhilarating without being challenging or terrifying. At one point a chasm in the rock face was crossed with the aid of a wooden walkway that swung with every footfall but more wire ropes provided something to hold onto. We emerged onto a rocky ledge, dusty underfoot and with a steep drop on the right to the river below, and the rocky wall on the left curving up to make a ceiling above us. A dead tree clung to the edge of the cliff, its twisted polished trunk curving outwards and upwards. Living trees clung to the rock ledges along the sides of the canyon above and below us, many were dressed with pale yellowy green leaves. It seemed that every day brought more colour to the trees.

The path dropped back to the river and soon we were not alone. A black and white border collie, not a puppy but not yet an adult, dashed past us until a distance whistle had it running back to its owner somewhere behind us. We climbed up onto a very narrow rock ledge set back into the cliff face, carved into the rock it resembled an open sided tunnel. Wire ropes fixed into the wall gave unnecessary reassurance although the ledge was no more than a foot wide at times. How would the boisterous dog manage on this narrow shelf? We soon had an answer as, whilst Mike was taking photographs, the man and his collie appeared on the ledge. The dog was not on a lead, perhaps as well, one wrong giddy move and it could have pulled its owner over the edge or risk being strangled, but it was quite obedient to his commands as he kept it near and guided it close into the cliff face.

Now the river was no wider than a few feet, possible to jump if you were feeling reckless. The sides of the canyon pressed in and the grey blue river glided silently between massive rock faces and boulders worn smooth by countless gallons of water over countless centuries. At other places in the canyon it was easy to judge the depth of the river, with often the pebble covered bottom visible, but here it could reach to considerable depth forced downwards by the constricting sides of this narrow part of the gorge. In places tree trunks and branches had been carried down by the swollen river and were now jammed between the rocks and boulders.

We reached a signpost: this was where we would leave the canyon. But the footpath still continued to follow the river for a half a kilometre or so until it could go no further. Not ready to end the riverside walk too soon and eager to explore as much as we could, we continued on the dead end path as it looped round a bend in the river, between trees shaded by steep rock walls. This was marked on the map as l'Imbut. We could go no further, the path petered out on a narrow rock and boulder strewn beach and we walked down through the trees to reach the river bank. Sentier l'Imbut exists as a work of persistent labour and engineering, for without the carved out sections of rock, without the metal work it would be impossible to walk this part of the Verdon Gorge. And here, on the rocky beach it was clearly apparent why the path ended where it did. The river disappeared under the rocks and boulders, slipping into a narrow gap that defied anything other than fish to follow. Boulders the size of buildings guarded the narrow bend in the gorge. We scrambled over a few hoping for a glimpse of the river as it emerged, and then we sat down in the quiet empty surroundings to have lunch. Mike scrambled further through the boulder field, ever the explorer and confident of his abilities as a once keen climber. I was put off by the huge gaps that opened between the boulders, black seemingly bottomless shadows, and the thought of falling into the gaps never to get back out, limbs broken, specs knocked askew and chocolate uneaten.

We had seen no further sign of the dog and his owner as we retraced our route to the signpost and the path up out of the canyon. If I wondered how the dog had coped on some of the narrow ledges, what came next would surely have posed even more of a challenge. The road was over a thousand feet above us and the climb out almost sheer. The first part of the path was a mixture of climb and scramble up through trees and dry soil that slipped and moved underfoot. Then we reached the cliff face. A narrow path, part steps part steep slope had been carved into the rocks and once again the comforting wire hand rail was bolted into place. We climbed, Mike in the lead, stopping every so often to take photos of me posing on the cliff face. The images show me looking up, head tilted back, towards the camera, the grey and orangey pink rock face stretching away beneath my feet. We were now above many of the trees that grew in the narrow stretch of this part of the gorge, looking down onto the top of their canopies and further to the river far below. If you suffered from vertigo this would not be the walk for you. If I had just been standing on the narrow ledge with nothing to hold on to it might have been a little more frightening, but with the wire ever present it was reassuring. Ladders however are a different matter – I painted the gutters and the bedroom windows once at home – each brush stroke took ten times as long as normal because I was scared to move. After that I vowed that next time I would employ someone, DIY is fine but extreme DIY? No thank you.

So there I was remembering with dread the gutter painting episode, when I rounded the corner of the cliff face and nearly walked into a ladder. Not just one but several, one above the other, stretching away up the vertical rock face.

"You'll be fine," reassured Mike.

But I had my doubts, and the uncertainty was made worse because, part way up the ladders and clearly not enjoying themselves one little bit, were two middle aged couples. It was quite obvious they were struggling with the height and the steepness and so we waited for them to reach the top of the ladders before we began our own ascent. Had the dog come up here? Could dogs climb ladders? I know cats can because much to my terror my own cat had tried to get involved when I was painting the windows. I'm not sure what had been more worrying: realising she was climbing up the ladders behind me or watching as she turned and ran head first back down them!

Anyway, the ladders became free and with a quick "you okay?" Mike began to climb. I followed him but the anticipated terror didn't come. These ladders were actually quite enjoyable. Yes, I did say enjoyable, and no, the altitude hadn't gone to my head. Whether it was because the ladders were firmly bolted to the rock face and not flexing with every step like the ones at home had done, whether it was because I wasn't carrying an open tin of paint and a brush, or whether it was because there wasn't a bonkers black and white feline stalking me, I'm not sure. But I got to the top rung of the first ladder and with a little shuffle stepped across onto the bottom of the second ladder just to the left of the first, and continued to climb. At least I knew we were not going to meet anyone coming down. This part of the trail was one way, and it needed to be, you could not have passed people on the narrow path never mind the ladders.

We soon reached the top of the path and came into woodland where boxwood grew in low clumps amongst the taller oaks. The two couples had gone to sit near the edge of the cliffs, looking down into the gorge as they took a rest and a drink. We left them and continued up   through the wood to the road. Crossing, we climbed some more, a less steep ascent this time that gradually drew us further from the road and into the leaf dappled sunshine of the warm afternoon. Three hundred feet higher than the road was a forest track that we emerged onto, turning left to follow it for a little way. Where a footpath left the track we turned off and began a gradual descent through the trees. In some places we broke out into clearings where wild plants were still in flower despite the late season, and blue tits and great tits sang in the branches. The bird song was the only sound we heard apart from an occasional car on the road nearby. When we reached the road itself we had a short walk along it before reaching the car park. Our car had been on its own when we had set out that morning but now the car park was full of cars, camper vans and a couple of motor bikes.

After the steep ascents and descents and the often rocky path it was a relief to take our walking boots off and slip our feet into comfortable trainers. We sat on the lip of the boot, gulping water and discussing what we should do for the remainder of the afternoon. We consulted the map and decided to continue along the road for views of the canyon and to reach a bridge that crossed the Canyon de l'Artuby a few miles further along. Mike had read something interesting about the bridge and seemed keen that I should see it.

The drive was a pleasant experience, more switch backs, more sharp bends and narrow curves and a couple of tunnels that cut through the rocks where it was impossible to drive a road around them.

"I'm glad there're not any motor homes about," I said pre-emptively.

As I rounded the next bend a motorhome appeared labouring towards me on the narrow road. I think the driver was relying on his size to get him through, although he realised at the last second that it would be him that went over the edge of the gorge, I would just have gone into the ditch. We slowed and squeezed past one another before breathing out again.

The car park at the side of the road just before Pont de l'Artuby was crowded with camper vans and cars. We pulled into the last remaining space and got out to walk onto the bridge. There seemed to be something happening in the middle of the bridge.

"What's that? Oh my god," I gasped. "Someone's standing on the parapet!"

"He's about to jump," remarked Mike very calmly.

This, as I quickly came to realise, was the famous bungee jumping site of choice for all thrill seekers and idiots in southern Europe. I watched with a certain degree of horrified fascination as the person in the middle of the bridge leapt off. He screamed all the way down, and most of the way back up, and then all the way down again, and then up again, and down until the elastic finally ran out of ping and he was lowered by means of a pulley on the bridge to the waiting paramedics below. Actually I think they were just employees of the bungee jumping company.

Unbelievably for me, more people were lining up to take his place, to step into his harness, to throw themselves off. Suppose the elastic broke? Suppose it stretched? (Was there a weight limit to this)? Suppose it was too long?

"I suppose you want a go now?" Mike asked with a grin.

"Merci aber non," I replied in my best Freman.

Mike rolled his eyes.

"What? What have I said?"

"Nothing dear," he sighed shaking his head.

I reviewed my comment. "Oh, is non not no?"

"No, non is no."

"Eh? Do you mean yes or no, non is no?"

"Non is no. Mais is but."

"I'm but?" I repeated. "You're confusing me now!"

"What?! It doesn't take much."

"You just said May is but."

"Yes, mais not May! Mais is but in French, you said aber!"

"Oh, that's but in German!"

"By George, I think she's got it."

We were just about to walk out onto the bridge when Mike was accosted by an elderly French couple waving their camera. With a series of gestures the lady indicated just how she wanted the photo taking as she posed with her husband against the parapet. Mike clicked the button and the lady rushed over to examine the image.

"No, s'il vous plait…"

More arm waving and smiling and gesturing followed as she realigned both Mike and her husband, and three photographs later she was finally happy with the result. With much effusive 'merci-ing' they left us and set off for the middle of the bridge.

"See, they are having a go!" grinned Mike.

"I'll have a go at you in a minute if you don't watch it!"

The French couple stood watching another person risk life, limb, back and retinas. Music was blaring from speakers set up by the jumping off point in the centre of the bridge, whether the music was intended to draw people in or mask the screams of the falling I'm not sure. We walked up to the jumping point, watching the careful preparations as yet another person paid to jump off into hundreds of feet of empty space on the end of what is basically just a wide bit of knicker elastic.

"I suppose it might help open up my vertebrae," I pondered, listening to the ear piercing screams of another willing victim. "However, for now I'll just keep doing the exercises the phyiso gave me."

I had trapped a nerve in my lower back a few weeks ago. Bending over without keeping my back straight was not pleasant, and had seriously restricted what I was currently able to do without causing a lot of pain. Cycling was currently off the menu which I was finding most frustrating, also on the list of things to be avoided were bending over to pick up dropped items, lifting heavy objects and vacuuming, so not all bad then. The only exception I had been able to make to this was when I dropped a bar of chocolate – that I had been able to pick up – anticipated pleasure overcoming short term pain.

Returning to the car, we drove over the bridge and up the road beyond a little way to a viewing area that overlooked la Mescala. The pebble beach where we had eaten lunch the day before was hundreds of feet below us and our lofty viewpoint provided wonderful views into the canyon on both sides of its sharp bend.

€-€-€-€-€

The next morning was our first cloudy day. Mike seemed in less of a tearing hurry to get up and so we had a more leisurely start to the day, strolling down to the boulangerie to purchase croissants for breakfast. There is only one bakery in Moustiers Sainte-Marie, bit of a shame really as it had not yet opened when we reached it that morning. In fact, we only ever saw it open once and that was the day we arrived when we had been to the supermarket and were in no need of it. A patisserie just around the corner was closed and up for sale, so that wasn't much help. My pre-holiday dreams of daily gateaux were not to come true. Fortunately for us, and possibly because the owner had seen a gap in the early morning baked goods market, another shop which doubled as an ice cream take away was open early each morning and sold baguettes, croissants and pain au chocolat. So we became regular early morning customers, usually buying a baguette for lunch and breakfasts of croissants for Mike and pain au chocolat for me.

Entering the shop for the first time we quickly debated what to purchase. Two baguettes would be better than one and feeling confident I could order the items I took the lead.

"Bonjour," said the shop keeper.

"Bonjour," we replied.

"Un pain au chocolat s'il vous plait," I began confidently enough.

The shopkeeper bagged a pain au chocolat and placed it on top of the counter.

"Et un croissant s'il vous plait."

So far so good. But then my mind went blank. What was two in French? The shopkeeper was waiting expectantly. Mike hovered at my side with a quizzical look on his face.

"Er, baguette, er…" I mumbled.

"Have you forgotten how many we want?" asked Mike.

"No! I've forgotten my French! Shush, I'm counting. Un, deux. Deux! That's it!"

Mike began laughing and rolling his eyes, the shopkeeper smiled.

"Deux baguettes s'il vous plait," I grinned triumphantly.

The shopkeeper bagged everything up and then told me the price. At which point I just got completely lost. I had been attempting to add things up as we went along and thought the total was €3.80 but that certainly didn't sound like the price the shopkeeper was asking for. I glanced at the cash register which was displaying €3.80. Was I hearing things? Misunderstanding? Surely not! But it sounded like the shopkeeper had asked for four somethings. Confused and anxious not to embarrass myself further I simply handed over a €5 note and took the offered change.

"I don't understand that," I remarked as we left the shop and began strolling back up the lane to our apartment.

"Which bit in particular? Or do you mean all of it?" chuckled Mike.

"No the numbers bit. I thought he said four. Quatre's four isn't it? Or have I forgotten that too?"

"Yes, quatre is four. Well remembered!"

"But it didn't add up to four," I protested, mightily confused.

"He said quatre-vingts."

"Van? What's van?"

"Vingts not van! Vingts is twenty."

"Oh, well, you're just making things worse now! There was no twenty either." Adding, as I began to get suspicious, "Are you winding me up?"

"No," laughed Mike, doing that eye roll thing again, if he did it much more I'm sure they'd fall out! "The French don't have a specific word for eighty, they say four twenties instead."

"What?!" I exclaimed. "I remember that in French you say one and twenty for twenty one. But four twenties! That's just bonkers. It's like speaking, well, a foreign language. Which it is, come to think about it. Four twenties. How daft."

"So I don't suppose you know the French for ninety?" he grinned.

"Oh, don't tell me! It's got to be three thirties, or six fifteens, or something equally mathematical!"

"Quatre-vingts-dix."

"Four twenty, hang on, un, deux, trois, quatre, cinq, six, sept, er... acht, neun, no that's wrong..." I hesitated.

"You've switched to German!" declared Mike, doing a bit more eye rolling and nearly doubling over with mirth.

"Oh, I give up. What is it? Quatre-van whatever you said?"

"Ninety is four twenties ten."

I glanced sceptically at him. He looked fairly serious.

"Are you serious?" I asked.

"Yep!"

"Bloody hell," I muttered. "It's worse than Roman numerals. One very excellent little car drives miles."

"What?" Now it was Mike's turn to look puzzled.

"It's a whatsit to help remember what the Roman numerals stand for. And at no point is there a four twenty ten!"

Breakfast over and quick lesson in counting in French delivered, we left the village heading for the northern side of the Verdon Gorge and parked in a small car park at la Colle de l'Olivier to walk the circular Sentier de Pecheurs or Fisherman's Path. This was a shorter and much easier walk than either of the previous gorge walks we had undertaken, running for a little over three miles on much gentler tracks down into the western end of the gorge. A pleasant rocky path descended gradually through trees bursting with autumn foliage. The trees suddenly cleared and we found ourselves on a grassy plateau between the gorge and the road. Tucked up against the edge of the road was the empty, graffiti-covered building that had once been the home of the road mender. Plateaux like this are not uncommon in the area and were often used to grow crops or keep flocks of sheep or goats or a few cows. There were no animals or crops on the plateau but as we followed the path dropping off the edge of the plateau we came upon two chamois with their distinctive brown bodies and pale, striped faces. They seemed unconcerned by our sudden arrival, one moving slowly away from the path, the other remaining sitting on a small ledge watching as we went by.

Shortly after leaving the plateau, at a point where the trees grew closer together forming a shady area, we reached a small cascade and cave. The water running over the rock surface had laid down deposits of tufa in smooth, rounded formations. Tufa is a form of limestone, and is formed in much the same way as stalagmites and stalactites are formed in caves, with the carbonate minerals precipitating out of solution to build up on top of previous deposits. The rounded rock face above the cave was similar to a larger one formed in the same way that sat on the other side of the road above the road mender's house. In the darker woodland, this rock face was covered in a deep layer of brown and green moss and algae. At this time of year there was just a trickle of water that ran between the rounded stones in front of the cave. It was one of the few places we actually got our boots muddy in Provence.

We reached the river after a gradual descent and turned left, changing direction to begin the walk upstream that would take us back to the car. This was a wider part of the gorge and the river here was quite wide too. Cormorants stood drying their wings on the rocks, sometimes we saw one swimming on the surface before diving gracefully for fish. Under the far bank a group of mallard ducks swam about, dipping underwater for vegetation to eat. Every so often a cormorant would fly past, wings flapping silently and travelling close to the surface of the river.

As we neared the end of the walk and therefore the car park, we began encountering more people, families and couples taking advantage of the good weather and the autumn colours. Closer still to the car park we encountered a much less pleasant

105

scenario: litter. There had been very little litter on the paths up until then, a nice change from the amounts I've often found at home. But so close to the car park there was one type of litter that although biodegradable was particularly unpleasant, and that was tissues and toilet paper and sometimes the solid forerunners of the toilet paper. Mike commented that the French seem to make a habit of pooing outdoors, something that he had come across often in the French Alps. I don't like litter in any form. If you carry it in then you should carry it out, or in the case of toilet products at least bury them! Of the few amounts of litter we did see in Provence, most consisted of tissues and loo roll. Men don't need toilet paper most of the time but for women I know it's not too pleasant to have damp knickers. But what I can't understand is why you can't put it in a plastic bag and carry it out with you to dispose of properly. You'd do that for dog poo. In our soggy British climate the paper does disintegrate relatively quickly, although I still think it is horrible to find it lurking behind a wall or under a bush, but in the dry climate of Provence the paper takes much longer to break down. That, combined with the numbers of walkers on the busy trails, meant that we were constantly coming across vast amounts of tissue and toilet paper wherever there was a slight bit of cover on the paths.

We made sure to have lunch that day before we got too near to the car park and the litter, sitting instead on a rocky platform that provided excellent views back down the gorge. The spicy chorizo in the baguette was made all the tastier by the addition of a little wild thyme that I found growing where we sat.

After lunch we continued along the road, a pleasant drive to La Palud sur Verdon. The cloudy early morning had given way to a sunny day and we headed off through the village onto the Route des Cretes a twisting, turning, hairpin bend of a road that follows the northern side of the canyon. There were numerous laybys along the route and we stopped at nearly all of them, often in a convoy of tourists, seeing the same people at every view point. The views down into the canyon and along the gorge from the various points were staggering. Often metal railings would guard the edge of the cliffs, marking sheer drops to the river far below.

Huge birds glided over the gorge, dozens of them, sometimes swooping close by, sometimes disappearing into the distance or dropping down into the gorge, taking every advantage of the thermal air currents rising up from the gorge and the sun-warmed rock faces. Every so often a bird would give one slow, deep wing beat before continuing to glide. These magnificent birds were Griffon vultures and many people were patiently waiting to take photographs as they soared past. Several people were weighted down with camera equipment and long telephoto lenses. I felt quite inadequate as we snapped away with my little Panasonic.

The Griffon vulture is the largest raptor in Europe, with a colossal wingspan of between 2.5 – 2.8 metres, if you prefer that in old English that's between 8 and over 9 feet. Or put another way, if one was sitting in the middle of my kitchen it would not be able to fully open its wings. Not only are the wings long, they are broad too, they need to be to keep these huge creatures in the air. Seen from below, backlit by the sun, they appeared uniformly dark brown although their bodies and wings are actually mid brown and the flight feathers darker brown. When one soared close beneath us we could see that their upper bodies are buff brown and their heads and neck a very obvious white with a white Elizabethan ruff of feathers. The birds live in colonies of around ten to twenty pairs, building their nests on cliff ledges. They feed off carrion, the 'clean-up crew' of the Verdon as one book described them. Standing watching the dozens and dozens of these graceful birds soaring over the gorge it was hard to believe that they had died out by the end of the nineteenth century. That old story so typical of many great raptors such as our own red kite, a combination of hunting and poisoning had decimated the population until eventually there were none left. The poisoning, unlike our red kites, had not been targeted specifically at the vultures, instead it was aimed at large mammalian predators such as wolves and bears, but vultures eat carrion and so had ingested the poison in the corpses of the bears and wolves. No one may have set out to poison the vultures but the result was the same. In 1999 twelve Griffon vultures were fitted with rings and transmitters and released into the Verdon. Within the following five years, ninety Griffon vultures were released in all and a breeding colony was formed. By 2002 the first three birds to be born flew the nest. So a success story, but it highlights once again how carelessly the actions of man can impact on the environment, and how long and how much effort is needed before these actions can be redressed.

The Verdon Gorge is renowned for its rock climbing and there are innumerable routes of various difficulties all along its length. Many of the vehicles parked in the laybys on the Route des Cretes were camper vans belonging to climbers who had travelled from countries across Europe to experience climbing in the Verdon. Mike stood for many minutes watching climbers making slow progress up the rock faces below us. Climbing does not appeal to me, but it was fascinating to watch the skill of the men and women who inched like ants up the limestone cliffs. As we lay on a slab of rock beyond the railings watching two climbers on the curving cliff face to our right, I realised there was nothing between my nose and another slab of rock hundreds of feet below. Suddenly it was like being back on the ladder with the cat and the tin of paint.

"Shall we go?" Mike asked, standing up and peering over the edge.

"I'm stuck," I replied pathetically.

"Is it your back?" he worried, full of concern.

"No! It's the drop!"

Next thing I knew hands were firmly grasping my ankles and I was being dragged back away from the cliff edge. I didn't care that I was scrapping my chin on the rock or that I was getting a liberal coating of white dust all down my front, I was just glad to be rescued. I dusted myself down and glanced around hoping my ignominious exit from the rock had not been noticed by anyone.

We continued along the Route des Cretes, cresting the highpoint before descending on an equally long series of switch backs and hairpins. Along this stretch the road was one way only, presumably to avoid a couple of oncoming campervans from driving one another over the edge. It did mean I didn't have to worry about taking the bends too sharply and as such I got to keep one eye on the scenery for some if not all of the time (think of the €700 insurance excess)! Near Chalet de la Maline the road became two way once more. It still wiggled alarmingly and narrowed at every bend when really you could have done with it widening, but at least the drop into the bottom of the gorge was now only three hundred metres or so, much more survivable obviously! At the Ravine de Mainmorte the road headed north back to La Palud where we re-joined the main road and continued back to Moustiers.

Entering the outskirts of the village we decided to call in at the supermarket. We're not talking a massive retail outlet one here: think more expanded corner shop. It was the end of the afternoon, the nice bread had all gone, the fresh milk was represented by one litre that was close to its use by date, but at least there were biscuits and beer! Mike spent ages choosing two bottles of local brew without realising they were made using honey (feeling very superior later that evening I pointed out that the odd flavour could have something to do with that word 'miel' printed on the label).

Knowing we would soon need more milk and beer, we checked the opening hours displayed on the door as we left the supermarket. Open tomorrow. That was good. A smaller (was that possible?) version of this supermarket was due to open in the old village later in the week, and remembering Norway I was determined we would not run out of essentials.

Tomorrow came and the supermarket was shut despite what the notice on the door said. The beer situation was okay, the chocolate was not in any danger of running out, but biscuits, bread, milk and provisions for more meals later in the week were not looking so good. At some point during the day we would have to find a shop somewhere.

It was another cloudy morning, our planned walked to the top of one of the nearby mountains was therefore put off for another day. If we were going to walk up a big hill then we wanted to be able to see some views when we reached the top instead of low cloud, rain and the inside of our cagoule hoods every time we turned our heads!

So with a long consultation of map and guide books and another pot of tea we eventually decided on a low level day of lake, villages, dams and hydroelectricity. Leaving Moustiers we headed down the shallow valley towards Lac de Sainte Croix and crossed the bridge to follow the road around the southern shore of the lake. This is France's largest reservoir and third largest lake. It sits on what was the plain of Les Salles-sur-Verdon. Back in 1908 a man called Georges Clemenceau had an idea of flooding the valley but his plans were shelved. In 1973 after much surveying, and considerable consternation on the part of the locals, the Verdon River at the western end of the valley was dammed, the land flooded and the village of Les Salles drowned. The lake holds 760 million cubic metres of water, which, to give it television media's favourite means of comparison, is the equivalent of 304,000 Olympic-sized swimming pools. That's a lot of lengths even for Michael Phelps! With all this potential water power sitting behind it, the hydroelectric dam is able to generate 150 million kWh every year. All of which is staggeringly impressive – but what about the poor folk of Les Salles who had been less than impressed with the plans? Well their village, now called Les Salles-sur-Verdon was rebuilt a little further up the valley side, it can claim to be the newest village in France, and having driven through it that morning I think it can claim to be the dullest too! Characterful it was not.

The road from Les Salles twisted inland before coming back to the lake at a narrow inlet where a side road led to another village, Bauduen. We drove down into this much luckier village, this too had been due for drowning in the original plans but had survived by just a few inches of water level. Tourist shops and cafes lining the shore were just opening for business and, climbing the hillside above, houses and a church looked down over the lake.

The lake itself is a bright azure turquoise blue, almost the colour associated with glacial lakes, the colour being the result of the clay bottom. Its creation undoubtedly had unwanted consequences for many of the locals but today it brings in money and tourists and many locals make a living from the water. There are numerous companies offering boat hire in the form of sailing, canoeing, kayaking and pedalos, although motor boats are not permitted. It is possible at the eastern end of the lake to take pedalos and other small craft into the gentler reaches of the Verdon Gorge. At every lakeside village there are swimming spots, picnic areas, campsites, cafes and food vendors. Specialist companies offer guided activities from walking and canyoning to white water rafting and climbing. There are even companies kitted out to take people who are wheelchair bound on walks in specialist contraptions that look like a cross between a sedan chair and a recumbent bicycle.

What old Blacas would have made of the huge lake where once a river meandered through a fertile valley is anyone's guess. Would he have been reassured to see a star still hanging about Moustiers? And would he have been frustrated like ourselves to discover the grocery shops don't open on Sundays and stay closed for two hours at lunch time? And as for his reaction to a concrete dam that makes invisible power using the flow of water! Man's ability to change and shape the planet is both incredible and destructive but it is also nice to realise that some aspects of our way of life have changed little over the centuries.

As we drove west from Bauduen we passed olive grows that would have been familiar to Blacas, and a little further along we stopped at the sleepy hilltop village of Baudinard-sur-Verdon. In summer places like these must be busy with tourists but in autumn it was difficult to imagine how the little café would make a profit that day, the only people drinking there were a waiter and the chef. A bill board advertised a sign for a supermarket, not here surely, it was too small? No, closer reading of the advertisement revealed the supermarket was twenty kilometres away.

The morning was turning into a tour of villages and we headed south and west towards Artignosc-sur-Verdon. The woodland gave way to agricultural fields for a while and near a junction we came to a place marked on the map as Fontayne where an ancient fortified farmhouse stood as a reminder of the troubled times of mediaeval Provence. From here the road looped down the hillside and into Artignosc. The wide main street was virtually empty, a lone workman was sweeping leaves and a couple of children cycled along the broad avenue lined with plane trees. A chateau marked one end of the village and a gated cemetery the other. The little villages of Provence are architecturally stunning and our day was turning into a pleasant day of easy sightseeing.

We returned to Baudinard-sur-Verdon and then drove downhill from the village and into woodland to emerge at an empty car park and picnic site opposite a field of lavender. We left the car, taking rucksacks containing lunch, and followed a trail through the woodland towards the Gorge de Baudinard. We were walking across bed rock, the white slabs of limestone worn smooth in places by feet and weather. Boxwood, oak and pines lined the path. The sun had yet to come out and the sky was a uniform grey. Robins flittered along the path in front of us, settling on a branch until we reached them and then flying a short distance away to land again and wait for us. The path descended gradually to bring us out overlooking the tree-lined banks of a small but wide lake in the river. Close to the water's edge birch trees were decked in pale yellow leaves, behind them darker leafed trees had yet to changed colour. Perched half way up the hillside on the opposite bank, the cream walls of the village of Montpezat stood out amongst the trees. Turning right we continued along the path that ran along low cliffs, the river had narrowed now as it ran through the Gorge de Baudinard. Jays chattered in the trees, the only sound in this peaceful landscape.

The sun was just beginning to break through the clouds as the path looped back on itself and we reached the car park. We had given our lunch a good walk, having failed to find anywhere comfortable to sit to eat it. Instead we changed out of walking boots and sat at one of the picnic benches to eat a lunch that once again consisted of baguette and chorizo.

"We need to find a shop that's open," I fretted, eating the last of the chorizo.

"I know, don't panic!"

"I'm not going to take any notice of you. When we find one, if we find one, we're stocking up on milk, biscuits…"

"Beer," interrupted Mike.

"Kaser."

Mike rolled his eyes.

"I mean fromage!"

"Oh! We should see if we can find any of that soft cheese we had in the Pyrennees."

"It stank."

"Yes, but it tasted nice."

Work on the dam or Barrage de Sainte-Croix, to give it its French title, began in 1971. From the footpath we had had views of the dam, with the power station and a bridge crossing the river behind it. After lunch we set off to drive over the bridge and continue along the northern shore of the lake. Soon we reached another village that had escaped drowning, Sainte-Croix-du-Verdon. The road looped steeply down between the houses before running along the shores of the lake. We passed a shop but it was shut, as were the countless campsites that lined the lake shore. It would hardly be a quiet place to pitch your tent in the height of summer. Several places offering boat hire and sailing were ranged along the shore. We parked and followed the road for a little way, before turning off onto a rough path that ran along the edge of the lake. There is no continuous path all around this ten kilometre long lake, possibly due to the steep and rocky nature of much of the shore. However there are several paths that follow sections of shoreline, the longest being part of the GR99 that hugs a sweeping curve on the southern shore near the village of Bauduen. Our path was mainly on the shingle beach and weaved inland a couple of times to cross narrow inlets where almost dried up streams flowed into the lake. The sun had come out and the skies were clearing rapidly. In the distance at the far side of the lake the mountain we had intended to climb that day was now sitting free of cloud. In summer this place would be bathed in sunshine almost constantly, with temperatures in the thirties, and the beach would be crowded with holidaymakers sunbathing and swimming. We passed just one family that afternoon, enjoying a picnic and ball games on the beach.

€-€-€-€-€

Driving up onto the Valensole plateau we set off in the direction of Riez. The Plateau de Valensole, which takes its name from the town of Valensole, is the largest lavender growing area in Provence. It was not until the nineteenth century that lavender began to be cultivated here and today almost eighty per cent of the world's production comes from Provence. In July the plain is a sea of purple. The lavender is planted in long rows, striping the landscape. The grey green leaves of these dense, rounded plants were all that remained, the rich purple flowers having already been harvested for their oils which are used in soap making and perfumery.

The village of Riez sits in a river valley below the edge of the plateau and is officially listed as a village of character, to which I can attest, although compared to Moustiers it felt more like a town than a village. It is thought to be the oldest settlement in the Alpes de Haute Provence and has a long history. The Gauls settled here, then came the Romans in the first century B.C. building their town just outside the site of the modern town and leaving behind a legacy that remains to this day. We entered Riez through one of the old town gates, driving through a busy wide street lined with imposing buildings and shaded by plane trees whose upper branches had been heavily pruned to provide the tall trees with a stunted canopy. Fountains are everywhere in Riez, some dating back to the 1400s, some are attributed with having healing qualities. Riez is a popular spot on the tourist trail, partly for its history and architecture and partly for the many shops selling locally produced and sourced lavender, honey and truffles.

"Ooh! Supermarche!" I squealed, pointing to a sign that was plastered on a wall.

"It might be shut," cautioned Mike. "This is the middle of the afternoon afterall."

We found the supermarket relatively easily and, grabbing a few carriers from the boot of the car, set off for a bit of retail therapy, and some biscuits. French supermarkets are clearly no more trusting of their customers to return trolleys than English ones and I fumbled about looking for a one Euro coin to feed into the trolley lock. Mike had dashed back to the car to retrieve his rucksack, worried that our two carrier bags would not be strong enough to hold all the beer he was intent on buying.

The supermarket was well and truly open and crowded with locals. As with supermarkets at home the fruit and veg section was next to the entrance. Unlike supermarkets at home, ones on the continent very often have a system of weighing and pricing your own products before you get to the till. The one in Castellane had some scales, with lots of pictograms and a little printer that churned out sticky price labels for the customer to attach to their bags of fruit and veg before eventually taking all their shopping to the checkout. Accustomed to having goods weighed and priced at the checkout in Britain, we had fallen foul of the continental system whilst on holiday in

Switzerland and embarrassed ourselves deeply at the head of a long checkout queue. Ever since then we had been very careful to make sure we didn't repeat the experience. So having filled several plastic bags with peppers, tomatoes, apples, clementines and grapes we began to look about for the weighing scales and label printing machine.

"There isn't one," I muttered.

"There must be. What are other people doing?" Mike whispered.

We looked around but no one seemed to be doing anything other than selecting vegetables.

"Tell you what," suggested Mike. "I'll stay here and watch to see what everyone else does, while you go off and get the rest of the shopping."

"Okay."

Ten minutes later I was back, trolley laden with milk, biscuits and several cheeses including the soft one Mike had so coveted. Mike himself was looking most suspicious, lurking about the salad section and following other customers. With his swarthy complexion, bushy beard, wild eyebrows and rucksack I would not have been surprised if a member of staff or vigilant customer had not called a security alert and had him arrested and his rucksack blown up in a controlled explosion.

"What are you doing," I hissed, coming up behind him and dragging him away from a distressed looking elderly lady.

"I've not seen a single person weigh anything."

"Okay, well in that case we'll risk it at the checkout. Now, I've got you that smelly cheese but we still need some bread, meat and oh my god! Look at that!"

"Eh? What?" Mike asked spinning round in fright.

"Le grand gateaux!" I squealed in delight, getting odd looks from several customers.

Mike rolled his eyes. "What are you talking about?"

"There in this chiller. Some gateaux! We must get some," and with that I popped a delicious looking chocolate and cream confection carefully into the trolley.

"But what was all that 'grand gateaux' about?" asked Mike.

"Grrrrand gateaux," I repeated. "I was rolling my rrrr's!"

"Oh, that's what you were doing. Sorry, I thought you were doing an impression of someone from Somerset. It sounded more like The Wurzels do Provence!"

"The cheese can go back on the shelf you know!"

We finished off our shopping with not just bread and beer but a bottle of red wine, priced at an envy-inducing €3 and which Mike later declared to be 'most quaffable'. Our sausage casserole of the other evening had been so delicious we decided to repeat it and began browsing the meat section for the same smoked sausages. We failed to find them, perhaps because this different supermarket chain did not stock them.

"There are these Andrex sausage," I commented, pointing to a packet of thick, meaty, herby looking sausage. At the time I little realised how apt my grammatical error would be.

"What sausage?" Mike repeated, leaning in for a closer look. "Andouillettes!"

"That's almost what I said! Andouillettes Sup... Super... Superi... Superieures," I read, with difficulty.

"Well, they look okay, they aren't smoked but they'd be okay in a casserole."

So the sausages were added to the trolley and we made our way to the checkouts. The queue of customers, all of whom seemed to know one another, moved slowly forwards as they chatted to each other and to the cashier.

Our trolley load of shopping came to a reasonable €60 and we packed up carriers and rucksack and returned to the car. The supermarket had a petrol station and we took the opportunity to fill up, watching again what another customer did before committing ourselves to any more embarrassing episodes.

"Can we try and get rid of some of this loose change?" I asked counting handfuls of Euros and cents into my hand.

"How much do you want me to put in then?" Mike asked.

"Anything that ends in €4.86 would be good!"

€24.86 nearly filled the tank and we drove up to the cashier's booth to pay.

"Bonjour," she smiled.

"Bonjour," I replied, knocking the gear lever into neutral with one hand and reaching out of the window with the money in my other hand.

But the metal chute to place the money into was pulling ahead of us. Or it could have been the car was rolling backwards.

"Eeek!" I squealed, nearly dropping the money as I fumbled for a handbrake that wasn't there with my left hand. Wrong side! Wrong side! Mike came to the rescue, snatching the handbrake up just as I was slamming my foot on the brake.

The cashier was laughing unrestrainedly at our antics.

"Sorry," I apologised as I lined the car back up with the cash booth. "Er, I mean… what do I mean?"

"Pardonnez moi," Mike replied.

"Oh, yes, that's it! Pardonnez moi," I said to the cashier, making her smile all the more. Did she roll her eyes or was it just my imagination?

"She must think the English are idiots," Mike commented, laughing as we drove away.

It was late afternoon by this time and we were both looking forward to a cup of tea but there was one sight I was determined to find in Riez. The Romans left behind four Corinthian columns, all that remain of the Temple of Apollo built in the first century A.D., and we found them quite by chance as we were driving back through Riez. Parking the car next to another ancient monument in the form of the Merovingian baptistery, we walked across a field and over a tiny bridge to where these four towering columns stand alone in the middle of a field. Each column sits on its own stone plinth, and spanning the top of the columns are three huge rectangular shaped cap stones. The carvings on the tops of each column are still relatively fresh but the land around the columns has built up over the centuries to leave them sitting in a depression in the ground. An information board nearby illustrated how the temple and the Roman village might have originally looked. An elderly man had brought his deck chair out and was sitting in the sunshine looking towards the temple. We retraced our route to the car and the baptistery. This had been built in the fifth century, reusing much of the stonework taken from the old Roman baths, of which there was now no trace.

We headed back in the direction of Moustiers climbing from Riez onto the plateau and travelling on the fastest, straightest road we had yet found. Lavender fields and ploughed fields of bare earth were occasionally interspersed with woody copses. Before leaving the plateau we turned off to take a smaller road that ran along the edge of the plain, overlooking Lac de Sainte-Croix. The views across the lake were beautiful, with the wooded hillsides stretching away from the blue waters towards the bare white rocky slopes and cliffs of the mountains in the distance. At one view point opposite Moustiers we stopped to admire the setting sun lighting up the village, casting amber glows on the houses and roofs; the quality of the light was beautiful. As we stood there, watching the light change and taking photographs, a car drew up nearby and a couple got out and began to unload the boot, setting up a picnic table, complete with red gingham cloth, camping chairs, cutlery, crockery, wine and candles. We turned to leave only to find them sitting directly behind us and beginning to open the wine, almost as if they were waiting for us to leave so they could begin a rather upmarket al fresco supper whilst the sun set and they watched the moon rise above Moustiers.

Trees lined this road, bordering the lavender fields and they had shed numerous quantities of what appeared to be very round, green apples onto the verges and the edge of the road. We stopped to take a closer look. But these weren't apples.

"That's a walnut tree," exclaimed Mike, examining the bark of the trunk.

The green 'fruit' were the outer protective casings of walnuts. Taking a stone I bashed off some of the fleshy wet fruit to get to the shell inside. Whilst I hammered away at the shell and began to nibble on the nut Mike was busy peeling several more nuts from the green flesh. The nuts were delicious, if hard work to get to, but the nuts were not really worth the effort, particularly as the green fleshy outer casing stained our skin and nails dark brown. As we later discovered the stains resisted all attempts to wash them off.

"Someone should market this stuff as self-tan, they'd make a fortune," Mike commented, looking at his hands.

Back at the apartment we unpacked the shopping and made a pot of tea, relaxing with a biscuit before making plans for our evening meal.

"Pizza and salad?" suggested Mike.

"Or vegetable chilli?"

We opted for chilli and began chopping the veg and opening a can of tomatoes.

"There are four big sausages in this pack, we could use one in the chilli and still have enough for the casserole another evening," I suggested.

Mike seemed to think it was a good idea and I slit open the packaging with a sharp knife.

"Oh…"

"What?" he asked absent-mindedly, as he added some chilli flakes to the pan of tomatoes and onions simmering on the hob.

"These sausages smell like merde!"

"What?" Mike asked, clearly thinking I had got my French wrong again and coming over to examine the grey, speckled sausage that I had removed from the wrapping. "Oh, phew! I see what you mean."

The smell coming off the sausage was quite distinctive and not a bit like the smell of the smoked sausages we had eaten a few days previously. If anything it resembled the smell from the fields at home after the local farmer has been muck spreading. Now at this point, any couple with an ounce of sense might have decided to cut their losses and put the

127

sausages in the bin. But no. Whilst I began to cut the sausage into slices Mike tried to translate the list of ingredients on the packet of sausage.

"I'm not sure what this means," he muttered, peering over the top of his glasses at the tiny print.

"There's bit in English that says 'if you can't read this you need to visit the opticians'," I teased.

But really this was no laughing matter. The slices of sausage gave no further clue to their contents and we optimistically tipped them into the pan of perfectly good vegetable chilli. Now looking back, I think my rational at that point was that if they didn't taste too good we could fish the slices of sausage out and not eat them. However, the slices of sausage had other ideas and they immediately disintegrated. Fishing them out was no longer an option. I stirred the chilli with increasing trepidation as the smell of spicy poo began to fill the apartment and Mike hastened to open a window. At one point a rather filamentous bit of grey flesh clung to the wooden spoon and I lifted the spoon out of the pan for a closer look. If I didn't know any better I would have said I was looking at the villi-covered lining of some part of the alimentary canal. The word 'tripe' surfaced briefly in the back of my mind, in a similar manner to the way various odd bits of grey flesh were surfacing in the pan of chilli.

Now having been married for seventeen years to a man who was neither big on hygiene nor cooking, I have long been wary of what I'm putting into my mouth. So I can only put it down to an uncharacteristic bit of culinary adventurousness, or possibly too much unaccustomed sun, but the next moment I found myself opening my mouth and putting the grey bit of flesh in. I was in a foreign country, I was trying to embrace the culture, the language (granted with varying degrees of success), the cuisine, and so I was curious to know what it tasted like. Poo, that's what it tasted like! Actually I'm assuming it tasted of poo, never having eaten poo. I chewed, my teeth seemed to bounce off it and then I swallowed.

"Pasta's ready," said Mike, and began draining a pan of pasta and selecting some plates from the cupboard.

I dished up in silence. We ate in silence. Somehow. Every so often I would land a forkful of something that I had last seen in an episode of Alien Autopsy. Mike cleared his plate, but although I ate all the veg chilli and the pasta the edges of my plate were rimmed with strange grey body parts by the time I finished eating.

My mum grew up during rationing. So I was raised on the premise of 'waste not, want not'. And to this day I don't like to waste food. However, sometimes you have to make an exception. The remaining three sausages went out for a walk with us later that evening, we walked round the village and up to the Chapel, the sausages only went as far as a litter bin in the square.

It was not until we returned home and went on the internet that we determined just what those Andouillettes Superieures contained: pigs' stomach and large intestines. So it was indeed villi I had seen. Little wonder the sausages smelt of merde! I know we eat tripe in England, I'm from Lancashire the home of tripe, although I don't indulge myself; and I'm all for making use of all the animal if we're going to kill it to eat. But surely that's where pet food comes in?

Much to my surprise the sausage chilli stayed down, although I had a few bizarre dreams that night. The next morning, feeling in need of something a little less adventurous we had toast and bilberry jam for breakfast. Mike opted for his smelly cheese in a baguette for lunch, I like the taste of this particular soft cheese but find it too rich in anything but small quantities, so I made myself a tuna mayonnaise baguette for lunch.

The day was another clear blue sky day, ideal for walking up the mountain and so we set off loaded with plenty of water, sandwiches, fruit and chocolate for the active day ahead. There are various routes up Les Grande Marges one starting at Aiguines and another on the road close to the exit of Sentier l'Imbut. We had decided to take a shorter route which cut up from the road between these two routes, with our stay in Provence limited this shorter option would enable us to walk up this mountain in the morning and do another walk in the afternoon.

Leaving the car in a small layby on the road high above the southern side of the Verdon Gorge, we set off climbing a steep, narrow path between low boxwood and scrub, quickly gaining altitude as we entered a beech wood. Beech masts crunched and skidded underfoot on the loose soil and russet leaves rained down on us from the branches above. We left the beech trees, still climbing to emerge on a gentler slope where pine trees grew amongst more boxwood and juniper shrubs. The soil was thinner here, the plant types reflecting this. Soon we joined the path coming up from Aiguines and followed it to the summit of Les Grande Marges some 1576 metres, nearly 5200 feet, above sea level. The views were astounding, behind us the blue stretch of Lac de Sainte-Croix, to the north and east the dim peaks of the Alps and immediately below our feet, dropping away down the rocky slopes, the Verdon Gorge. We sat admiring the view and having a drink before retracing our steps to the car far below.

€-€-€-€-€

It was hardly worth changing our footwear as we drove back down the mountainside, through Aiguines, across the bridge and turned onto the road signposted for La Palud-sur-Verdon and the northern side of the gorge. We parked only a little way from the end of the gorge and crossed the road to begin climbing the hillside to reach our eventual goal of Crete l'Issioule. The first part of the path was steep, through mixed deciduous trees, the soil dry and dusty underfoot. A small herd of wild goats were crowding the path at one point, grazing the shrubs and looking rather surprised to see us. They meandered off with little concern for our presence. Where the path levelled out for a short distance, giving views into the canyon, we stopped for lunch, sitting on a sun warmed rock and looking across the gorge and up to the summit of Les Grande Marges. As Mike opened his rucksack to retrieve our lunch we were greeted with a waft of pungent cheese. We ate the baguettes and some of the chocolate, saving the rest and the fruit for later.

From this rocky ledge the climb began in earnest, an uphill slog through alternating patches of sun and shade as we walked between the trees. Near the top of the first part (not that I realised at that moment that there was a second part) the path skirted an overhanging cliff of creamy white limestone and the glade beneath was filled with the sound of a thousand buzzing insects. Wild bees were collecting nectar from the small clumps of plants that grew sporadically across the rock face. It was as if an adventurous gardener had climbed the cliff face to plant it at random with patches of bedding plants.

We continued up through the wood, emerging onto a cliff top that wasn't the top, and followed this along for a while before climbing once more, a shorter climb this but equally steep. Mike was leading when I became aware of someone close behind me. I turned to find a woman, older than I, almost on my heels. Where had she come from? I stepped to one side, apologising (in English of course!) for getting in her way and she passed with a smile and a 'merci', breaking into a run as she past Mike. I'm reasonably fit, at a steady pace we were climbing comfortably. But running? I'm always in awe of anyone that has the energy, fitness and stamina to run, especially uphill. And I'm also, I have to admit, somewhat jealous of their knees. My knees would soon be feeling the strain of the many downhills I was subjecting them to that week.

We emerged from coniferous trees onto the edge of Crete de l'Issioule, and suddenly all the sweat and effort was worthwhile. Following the way-marked trail we were soon on the line of the cliff edge. The landscape fell away below, the forest, the rocks, the gorge, the lake. Above: clear blue skies and numerous gliding vultures. To our left, the land rose gradually to mountains on the horizon, deep hidden valleys between us and further mountains, some of which we would walk up on other days. We sat, enjoying the view, the vultures and some more chocolate before setting off back the way we had come. When we reached the forest, instead of dropping down the steep slope we carried straight on, climbing slightly through the woods and continuing along the Crete de l'Issioule for a while. We disturbed some chamois that bounded quickly away through the trees.

At a different path beyond some power lines we turned off the main track and began a gradual descent. Although gradual, this descent was still challenging as for much of the way the path was little more than loose rocks, dust and gravel. My feet slid out from under me several times and I descended in a mess of pin-wheeling arms, skidding feet and squeals of terror. It was very thankfully that we finally reached a better, more level path at Bois de Felines, or cat wood. No cats but plenty of trees. Plenty of crickets too and birds, singing in the long grass and in the trees. Soon we reached the car where we gladly removed our walking boots and sat down in the shade to eat an apple.

Moustiers Sainte-Marie was busy with people as we arrived back that evening. The main tourist season might be over but French locals from near and far come to the village to appreciate the scenery, the history and the faience ware just as foreign tourists do. The crowds on the cobbled streets, browsing and window shopping in the gift shops and galleries and enjoying a drink and a snack at the cafes and bars reminded me of being in Haworth. The sun was just setting as we let ourselves into the apartment, put the kettle on and went upstairs for a shower and change of clothes. Sausage casserole was off the menu; instead we popped a mushroom pizza in the oven and prepared a salad.

I had read every bit of information I could find in the apartment, well, the English bits anyway, and discovered listed in the rental documents that somewhere there was a salad spinner. Great fun salad spinners. But where was it? Having searched every cupboard in the little kitchen, which did not take long, I eventually found it under the sink. Obviously.

"What's that?" asked Mike, never having worked in a sandwich shop he had been denied the joys of the salad spinner.

"It's a salad spinner," I replied, demonstrating this wondrous kitchen aid.

"That'd be good for drying my socks!"

"Don't even think about it!"

But we didn't need to resort to spinning our smalls in the kitchen ware, or (as I have sometimes done on walking holidays) drying our undies on the hot kettle. This apartment had a washing machine and, whilst laundry is not high on my holiday to-do list, it was very useful to have the facilities to do our washing as it had meant we need only take (and pay for) one piece of hold luggage. We had struggled at first to use the washing machine, an unfamiliar top loading specimen which came with lots of dials and programmes and of course lots of French wording. Picking which programme to use had not been too onerous but actually figuring out how to start the cycle was another matter. I was just about to give up and go and do some hand washing when, with a frustrated final turn of the dial, Mike brought the machine to life. There was no dryer but that was not a problem in the dry Provence climate, damp laundry draped over the clothes rack dried within a day even without any heating on in the apartment. Oh to have such a climate at home!

Arriving at the car early the next morning, en route to another day of walking in the gorge, I was surprised to trip over a pear. Where had that come from? Then I spotted another a little further across the car park. I was just about to point it out to Mike when a pear appeared rolling down the hill from the upper car park and came to rest at our feet. The pear was rock hard, so not worth taking with us to supplement lunch but, curious to find out where they were coming from, we walked up the road until we were suddenly almost hit by another pear. The source of the pears then became obvious. A pear tree in the top car park was shedding its fruit which were then falling into the road, bouncing off obstacles and into the gutter and then rolling down the hill to the lower parking area in a crazy game of pear pinball.

That morning we parked at Chalet de la Maline to complete the Sentier Martel out to La Mescala and back. We were there relatively early but already a white minibus was parked at the side of the road. Was it the minibus from the other day? We could hear a noisy group of walkers setting off down into the gorge. Hopefully they would soon get ahead of us and we could enjoy the peace. By the time we had locked the car and were preparing to set off we could see the group through a gap in the trees as they rounded the footpath that wound down the side of a ravine into the gorge. They hadn't got very far and we were soon to catch them up. I admit to being a bit antisocial when it comes to walking, I like to enjoy the peace of a place, listen to the bird song, hopefully catch a glimpse of some wildlife, things you can't do

136

so easily if you are part of noisy group. So we were in a quandary whether to hang back and let the group get ahead of us, or try to pass them and open up a lead.

The choice was taken out of our hands when we rounded a bend in the path to find the group had stopped and were busy snacking, talking and standing in the middle of the path. The path was narrow and surrounded at that point with boulders. We approached the group who all stopped talking to briefly glance at us before continuing their conversation. No one even attempted to move to the edge of the path and make room for us to pass. They stood firm, something Marshal Petain would have done well to do back in 1940, and we had to squeeze past them; muttered 'excusez moi's' (in Mike's French – not just mine) had no effect. We had barely got past them when they set off behind us and we exchanged frustrated glances as we picked up speed trying to get away from them. We quickly left them behind as they seemed intent on regular path blocking breaks, although for much of the morning we continued to hear their voices echoing stridently along the canyon.

A more welcome group we encountered all wore the uniform of the French Army and were quieter, younger and fitter. Well, I thought so. Each khaki-clad soldier that passed us, in full battledress, heavy rucksack and sturdy boots, greeted us with serious if friendly 'bonjours'. I eagerly replied, (well I needed all the practice I could get), Mike's replies were not quite as enthusiastic as mine.

A little further along the path a large family of mum and dad and six children were stopped having a picnic. The parents and all the children called 'bonjour' as we passed. It was a common occurrence in France, that all the family, including young children, politely greeted other walkers.

The path was very pleasant, a relatively easy walk through oak woodland, where many of the older trees sported great burrs on their lower trunks. Acorns and oak apples, those curious growths caused by a particular species of wasp, littered the path. The trees in the shade at the bottom of the gorge wore more autumn colours, with nearly all having pale yellow leaves, and we stopped many times to admire the colours and take photographs of the leaves reflecting in the smoothly flowing river. It did not seem to be long before we arrived at the junction of the paths that marked the diversion down to La Mescala, and once again we took the lower path out to the shingle beach and the sharp river bend for lunch.

"I hope that group don't come down here before we have finished lunch," Mike grumbled.

"They're bound to," I replied.'

But miraculously they didn't and we had the idyllic spot to ourselves. Miserable antisocial sods that we are! We were expecting to meet the group heading towards us as we retraced our steps but we never did. Unbelievably they must have continued along the Sentier without diverting to La Mescala, missing one of the most picturesque spots in the whole of the canyon.

We were overtaken by the large family on our return route. Again they all exchanged greetings as they passed us where we had stopped close to the edge of the river to take some colourful photos of the leaves reflecting in the grey blue water. The mother was last in line and it seemed like she was about to stop to chat. Mike was a few feet away in the trees just below the path, and I dreaded the thought of trying to converse and showing myself up in the process.

"C'est beau," said the mother, stopping next to me.

"Err…" I mumbled, my mind had gone blank, not an unusual state of affairs, as I frantically tried to figure out what she had said and tried to formulate a response, any response, but my entire, if very limited, French repertoire had deserted me.

"Err…" I tried again.

The French woman smiled at me and it was at that point that Mike came to the rescue with a reply in French.

"Oh, English!" guessed the woman.

"Yes, I mean, oui, sorry, yes," I blurted.

"It is very beautiful, no?" she replied warmly.

"Oui," we chorused.

The woman continued on the path, bidding us enjoy the rest of the day. Mike grinned at me and rolled his eyes.

"I know, I'm hopeless!" I laughed.

"Endearing," he replied with a smile.

Back at the car we debated what to do next. La Palud-sur-Verdon was just around the corner and so we parked up in the little village and had a look round. There is not a great deal to look around to be honest, the guide books make little mention of this seemingly sleepy village cut through by the main road, but in the height of the season this is one of the bases for holiday makers and companies offering adventure activities. There are a few cafes, a grocer and petrol station, your quintessential seller of honey and lavender, a few narrow quaint side streets, several accommodation providers and a chateau that now houses an information centre.

A group of motorcyclists were crowded round the pumps filling their bikes and using the pay at the pump facility. It was just as well there was one because the grocer and filling station combination was closed for the lunch two hours. Not only was the door locked, the lights turned off and the sign in the window turned to 'ferme', but a conga line of trolleys

140

had been used to barricade the doorway. Serious about not having a disturbed lunch these French shopkeepers!

"Oh, I was hoping to get some more beer," moaned Mike.

"Well unless there's a pump dispensing le beurre you're out of luck!"

"I think you mean biere, beurre is butter," explained Mike. "And it's la not le."

"Eh?"

"Both biere and beurre are female, so the definitive article is la not le."

"You see, this is what I find most confusing about speaking a foreign language..."

"What, like English?" Mike chuckled.

"Ah, ah, Cumbria Man. How can some inanimate object be male or female or neutral? It's ridiculous. A male pen, a female chair, a male dog, a female cat, a male..."

"But that's just how they do it," interrupted Mike, rolling his eyes.

"But you can have a dog that's female that's male. And a cat that's male that's female. And what if you've had your pet neutered? Then you've got a situation where you're going to refer to your biologically male cat, which has been made neutral, as female!"

"Eh?"

"And in German," I persisted, "the word for girls is Madchen but any word in German that ends 'chen' is neutral so all girls in German are neutral. Which, come to think of it, might not have been a bad idea when Hitler was trying to get all the young pure Aryan women to breed."

"Julia! ..."

"I find it all very confusing. I think the best way to learn a language is to immerse yourself in it..."

"It's not worked for your English... ow!" As I hit him. (Not big on violence but sometimes...)

"I think," I continued, trying to ignore him, "if I lived in a country for a year..."

"Like England? Ow!!" (He wasn't a quick learner)!

"...Like here, for instance! I would master the language much better. And after a year..."

"Everyone in Provence would be speaking French with a Burnley accent!"

That time I hurt my knuckles.

Ɛ-Ɛ-Ɛ-Ɛ-Ɛ

It's a very windy road that drops down from La Palud
to Point Sublime and the nearby village of Rougon.
The village is small, so no shops selling le biere, or
bandages. As you drive up the quiet road leading into
Rougon the first thing you cannot fail to see is the
rocky buttress just to the right of the village, topped
with some battlements. The second thing you can't
fail to spot is the gleaming white walls of the porch
on the stone chapel. The small chapel, with its walled
graveyard, cypress trees and bell tower is an idyllic
little building. A carved wooden trough sits to one
side of the porch and notices pinned inside the porch
gave lots of information about various things, most of
which I didn't really understand. I would have liked
to have gone inside but the building was locked.

Leaving the car parked by the chapel and the
recycling bins, we strolled up the empty road in the
heat of late afternoon to have a look around the
village some few hundred yards from the chapel. The
by now familiar architectural style of tall houses, red
tile roofs, narrow winding lanes and a tiny central
square typified Rougon. We wandered through the
lanes, passing several cats, some snoozing, some
having a wash and one up a ladder doing some
painting, in the direction of the buttress, following a
path that circled round and up to the top of the
wooded limestone pinnacle. The last few feet were a
rocky scramble making full use of hand holds before
we were standing on the tiny fortified summit. The

buttress was actually split in two just below the summit and the two peaks had been connected at some point in the past by an arched stone bridge-like structure. Two empty flag poles stood on each half of the buttress. The village of Rougon had grown up around the little castle, and records of a settlement on the site date back to the ninth century, it first being recorded as Villa Rovagonis in 814. On one half of the buttress sat the remains of an old mediaeval castle. Standing there with commanding views along the road in both directions and into the Verdon Gorge, it was easy to understand why this rocky pinnacle had been fortified. It made an ideal lookout point and had been a fundamental strategic location during many of the conflicts in past centuries, making up part the ring of defensive fortifications surrounding Castellane.

We found ourselves driving back towards La Palud the next morning. It was a chilly start, the thermometer in the car reading one degree above freezing, as we crested the hill and began to descend towards the village, the valley below was blanketed with a sea of mist. Soon we were in the mist, a thick fog really that kept the speed down and the windscreen wipers busy as we negotiated the twists and turns of the road. We left the main road near Rougon and took a winding road that followed a beautiful route, climbing steadily through a series of sweeping bends that carried us around one side of a long valley. It was not the shortest way to our destination but the scenery was worth the detour. Steep rocky hillsides closed in on our right and the valley sides fell away to the left. On one section bordered by mature oaks we spotted a red squirrel leaping from branch to branch and tree to tree, I slowed the car, keeping level with this agile little bundle of cute and we watched the seemingly impossible leaps, the safe landings, the balancing act of tail and dexterity of body and paws.

The road was narrow with many warnings of ice, the drop into the wooded valley steep, and I found myself hoping the squirrel would be the only thing we encountered. Trees on the opposite sides of the valley blazed with autumn colours, from deep reds to palest lemons. Mike was repeatedly calling for a stop as he dashed to the edge of the road to take photograph after photograph, every bend in the road revealing another impossibly improved view. We were now behind Chateauneuf les Moustiers and could make out the line of the old Roman road and the dark cave entrance where Notre Dame Chapel was located.

The road ran out at a place marked on the map as Les Chauvets, which seemed to consist of nothing other than a chapel sitting on an embankment at the side of the road. I was in desperate need of some bladder emptying, having gone a bit overboard on the tea consumption at breakfast, five cups was possibly one too many but much to my chagrin another couple were already parked in the layby.

"We either need to set off quickly and put some distance between us or hope they leave before I get my walking boots on. Otherwise there might be an accident," I explained quietly to Mike.

145

"Well at least that group from yesterday aren't here," he laughed.

Just then we heard a roaring of engine and a clash of gears and a white minibus appeared round the bend and screeched into the layby. I glared at Mike as if he was personally responsible for summoning it.

"It can't be," he said with stunned disbelief.

But oh yes it was. We could already here the strident voices before the engine had been shut off and any doors opened.

"It's not the same group, is it?"

"It is," I confirmed. "And the guide is wearing the same grubby olive green T-shirt as yesterday!"

Now we had a dilemma. Did we race ahead, hoping to open up a gap so I could find a convenient bush to hide behind, or did we linger? The trouble is I was in no state to linger for long, and the other couple didn't look like they were going to move any time soon, the woman was now throwing a ball for their little terrier.

"May be the chapel is open," I suggested.

"You can't wee in there!"

"No! I mean the group might go and have a look in there before setting off!"

But they didn't. After a couple of minutes of standing in a straggling line calling to one another, the grubby-shirted group leader set off, taking the path we would be going on.

"Right! Graveyard!" I instructed Mike.

He's used to me looking round graveyards so he didn't demure and tagged obediently along behind. The graveyard was neatly kept, the grass mown and the flowers fresh. And best of all it had just been extended through the back wall and into a newly prepared piece of ground. I shot through the little wooden gate in the wall, and was much relieved to find I was hidden from view, both of the group and the couple. Much relieved.

"Can we go now?" asked Mike as I re-emerged into the main part of the graveyard.

"I just have," I smiled with relief.

The couple were still throwing the ball for their little dog as we emerged from the graveyard and turned up the dusty, stony track towards Provence's second highest mountain. Le Chiran stands 1905 metres high overlooking the surrounding ridges, hills and valleys, and only the nearby Mourre de Chanier is higher, although not much higher, at 1930 metres. Le Chiran might not be the highest but it has more to offer in the form of an observatory, an orientation table and a mountain hut.

Our walk would have an elevation of about two thousand feet but it did not seem like it as we followed a gentle gradient through open countryside towards a col where the landscape levelled out. We quickly caught up with the noisy group, once again they had stopped at a narrow part of the path as it climbed through thickets of gorse and juniper, we hung back until they set off again and a short while later at the start of the col we were able to overtake them. Another group were already at the col, having driven up in a couple of minibuses. Lazy of them, you might think, but no. This was a mixed group of disabled teenagers and able bodied adults and was being led by one of the companies we had seen advertising in Castellane. This company specialised in taking disabled people into the hills and on the trails, using the specially adapted wheel chairs I had noted earlier.

Grubby guide obviously knew the guide of the second group and they stopped to chat. We carried on, across the grassy plateau of the col and towards a signpost at a meeting of footpaths. The signpost indicated that we were half way between the chapel and the summit of Le Chiran, three kilometres in either direction. We paused for photographs by the sign, behind rose a steep slope, covered in yellow grasses, that led to the sharp ridge of le Grand Mourre, which in turn continued, climbing gradually to reach Mourre De Chanier.

Our route now began a fairly gradual climb that followed a wide dusty track as it zigzagged up to the summit of Le Chiran. The group were by now nowhere in sight, although we could still hear them. With luck we would have the summit to ourselves, plus I was beginning to think five cups of tea had possibly been two too many.

A metal gate was closed across the path at the entrance to a wired off compound just below the summit, and a comical cartoon sign of a nosey chicken gave some sort of warning that chickens were on the loose. We ducked under the gate expecting to see lots of chickens scratching about in the dirt but there were no chickens, presumably because there was no one at the hut, it was closed for the season. The observatory was also closed, not that it mattered. We walked towards the orientation board and stood reading the names of mountains and trying to line them up with the direction of the arrows.

"So those mountains are part of the Mercantour National Park," Mike said, shuffling round the table and looking across towards a distant line of mountains.

The views were long range and stunning, we could see right into the Alps to the north and east, across the flat Provence plains to the west, and south towards the Mediterranean. Closer at hand was a stunning limestone escarpment with steep cliffs on one side, and a grassy slope falling away gradually on the other. Behind it was a valley and another line of hills and, in the distance beyond those, the snow-capped peaks of the Alps. Fold after fold of mountains, valley after green valley, rocky upper slopes and summits. We were in the largest geological park in Europe: the National Geological Reserve of Haute (High) Provence. The reserve covers an area in excess of two thousand square kilometres, encompassing the Verdon Gorge and the mountains around us. As the name suggests, the remit of the reserve is the preservation of the rocks, fossils and the countryside of the region. The geology of the landscape is plain to see in every ridge, escarpment, steep sided valley and deep-cut river gorge and within the reserve thousands of fossilized plants and animals have been discovered as well as the fossilized footprints of birds.

The silence was absolute, a peace you rarely hear in Britain where you are never far from a road. A raven croaked a call as it flew overhead to land nearby, obviously familiar with the concept of food-carrying humans on this mountain top. Ravens are a rare sight unless you are up in the mountains or a paying visitor to the Tower of London. The largest member of the crow family, they are, surprisingly, larger than a buzzard, with bodies that are four inches longer, and a slightly longer wingspan that stretches over four feet. Unlike buzzards with their brown and grey mixed plumage, ravens are completely black, with a metallic sheen when seen in sunlight. These intelligent birds feed on a mixed diet which can include carrion, and they mate for life, a fact I always find very endearing. Their distinctive, deep croaking cry makes them easy to identify, as do the 'fingers' at the end of their wings.

We stood for many minutes enjoying the peace, watching the hopeful raven and taking in the fabulous scenery. Mike came and put his arms around my waist and mumbled something.

Glancing at my watch, I confidently replied, "Twenty past eleven."

Mike rolled his eyes, leaned away from me slightly and with an exasperated expression said, "What?"

"Le temps! Twenty past eleven. You asked me what the time was. It's twenty past eleven."

"I never mentioned le temps."

"Yes you did. That's what it means isn't it? Temps – time. Tempus fugit and all that!"

"Quelle heure est-il: what time is it?"

"I've just told you, twenty past eleven, well just gone by now. And stop rolling your eyes at me!"

"No, no, no," he said, with careful patience. "I said: 'je t'aime'."

"Je temp?" I repeated.

"No," he said, speaking slowly now. "Je: I. T': you…"

"I thought tu was you?" I interrupted.

"It is," he said, looking me right in the eye as if he was trying to make a particularly dim-witted imbecile understand him, (which at that moment perhaps he was). "If the verb begins with a vowel then you put take the vowel off the end of the word before and substitute it with an apostrophe. So: Je: I. T': you. Aime…"

"Eurgh!" I blurted out. "You've got some goo in the corner of your mouth!"

"Oh, for goodness sake!" snapped Mike, letting go of my waist and swiping angrily at his mouth with the back of his hand.

"What? Well, you had! Anyway, what were you trying to tell me?"

"Oh, nothing. Never mind, the moment's gone now!"

We walked towards the front of the observatory, shrugged out of our rucksacks and sat down to have lunch. An overpowering smell of soft cheese came from Mike's rucksack. I was on tuna mayonnaise baguettes that day and tried to sit up wind of Mike's fromage.

"So, tell me again," I persisted, taking bit of baguette and chewing hungrily. "Two vowels on two words next to one another cancel one another out?"

"Sort of," he sighed. "I think the phrase you need to learn most is 'je ne comprends pas'."

152

"Oh! I know what that means!" And then as the realisation hit, "oh, you cheeky sod!"

Mike chuckled and nearly choked on a bit of crusty baguette, serve him right.

"Shouldn't it be comprendez?" I asked.

"No, that's the verb ending for first person plural."

"You're trying to confuse me now aren't you?"

"Doesn't take much," he muttered.

"First person pleural... You mean 'we'?"

"Oui."

"It kind of makes sense. Comprendez, comprehend. Avez, have. Arrivez, arrive. Pardonnez pardon. Excusez, excuse." Blimey! It was all coming back to me, I was on a roll! "Passez, pass. Givez, give. Eatez, eat. You just add 'ez' to the end of the vowel?"

"What?"

"Can't we just add 'ez' to the end of a vowel?" I repeated, beginning to wind him up. "If I do that and speak with a French accent then I'm bound to be understood."

I think it was a relief for us both when lunch was over. Mike didn't have to listen to my bizarre take on

153

the French language and I could no longer smell his cheese baguette. As we set off to walk back to the car the noisy group were just arriving at the summit. It seemed like no time at all before we reached the plateau and began to walk through the colourful grasses, disturbing butterflies and grasshoppers as we passed.

There were a few more vehicles parked near the chapel as we descended the last few yards of stony track that came out onto the road but no one was around. The chapel was disappointingly closed but on walking up to the door we did at least see something of interest. Clinging to the stone wall above our heads was a lizard; it inched slowly up the rough faced stone, pausing to search for small insects as it went. We watched until it almost reached the top of the wall, becoming harder to spot, perhaps it knew of an alternative way into the building.

€-€-€-€-€

We had neighbours that day. They arrived during the evening, stumbling up the shared stairwell and going into the other apartment in the building. We heard the cheerful voice of Madame as she ushered them upstairs, saying something about the light bulb soon getting brighter as they groped blindly, as we had done, on the unfamiliar steep and curving staircase. She was correct the bulb did eventually get brighter, the trick was remembering to leave it on for several hours!

The layout of the building meant both apartments had living and kitchen areas on the same floor and separate internal stairs leading to a second floor but the other apartment then had a bathroom above our bathroom. It made for interesting acoustics in the shower. But as it transpired a few hours later it also made for interesting acoustics in the bedroom. I was woken by a bang, well, I thought sleepily, it made a change from the church clock. Mike however, was still asleep. Then there was another bang, followed by another and another. Our new neighbours had a noisy headboard and, unfortunately for me, quite a lot of stamina. Well, if it's not Dutch couples on campsites in Scotland it is French couples in a neighbouring apartment. At least the apartment walls were thicker than tent walls and I didn't have to listen to their vocalisations as well. Mike slept on. Eventually the headboard either split in two or was given some respite and I was just drifting off to sleep when the church clock chimed midnight.

"Uh!" groaned Mike, waking up. "Is the window open? That clock seems loud."

"How come that wakes you up?" I asked in frustration, "But you can sleep through our neighbours trying to break through the wall with a headboard?"

But I was talking to myself. Mike was fast asleep again. The next time we woke up the church clock and my synchronised mobile were both marking 7 a.m. I took a shower anticipating a stroll to the shop for a fresh baguette and croissants.

"I might put this pink T-shirt on," I mumbled, fumbling about in the dimly lighted bedroom and unable to find my favourite blue one.

"Good idea," Mike replied enthusiastically.

"Oh! Does it suit me?" I said somewhat surprised, he rarely notices what I'm saying never mind what I'm wearing.

"Nah," he replied absentmindedly as he hopped about trying to put a sock on. "The pink shows up well in photos. Good contrast with the background. Good for scale."

"Thanks," I sighed.

What can be nicer than a walk to the bakery to buy your breakfast, through quiet lanes just waking up to another warm, sunny day? Eating the croissants when you get back to your apartment, with freshly brewed tea for me and coffee for Mike, that's what. Then we were out once more, packed lunch in rucksacks for our last walk in the Verdon Gorge. The car was covered in dew, the sky a stunning bright blue, not a cloud in sight. Driving down the curving lane to the outskirts of the village we approached the supermarket and a hotel and restaurant.

"Dog!" shouted Mike.

"Pig!" I shouted back, not like him to be insulting so early in the day but I was determined to give as good as I got.

"No, a dog! There! It's about to cross the road."

I had been distracted by the menu board of the pizza restaurant on one side of the road and had failed to see an old Labrador approaching the edge of the pavement to the right. I wasn't going fast, having just come round a right angle bend at a junction but slowed further and came to a stop. The old Labrador stopped too, waiting at the edge of the pavement a few feet in front of the car. It looked at me, and I waved it across. Yes, I know, how stupid of me! Like the dog was going to understand me waving at it! But the dog was waiting for me. We sat there waiting for one another to go first.

"It's waiting for you," said Mike, sounding as astonished as I felt.

I put the car in first and pulled slowly away, keeping a careful eye on the dog, just in case it wasn't really waiting for me and was going to suddenly exhibit typical animal lack of road sense. But this old dog had plenty of road sense, he watched us drive by and we both watched in the car mirrors as the dog looked left and right, checking for any more traffic, before deeming it safe to cross the road. Maybe it had heard about the jay walking laws, after all we were not too far from the police station.

There are a limited number of footpaths in the Verdon Gorge and we had done all except the Sentier du Bastidon. This trail started from the Ravine de Mainmorte that runs south from La Palud-sur-Verdon, quickly entering the Verdon Gorge proper and running roughly west along the northern side of the gorge some height above the river level before finally re-joining the Moustiers to Palud road several kilometres later. We would be making this into a spectacular circular walk by returning to Palud and then back to the car via a higher level route through woodland on the Cime de Barbin, a total distance of sixteen kilometres.

As we neared Palud, the valley beyond was cloaked in mist once again. It must be a regular occurrence in the cold autumn mornings. We turned right at Palud, descending the gentle hill towards the gorge, but before the road turned to run parallel to the gorge in the direction of Chalet de la Maline, we stopped, parking in a layby close to the start of the Sentier de Bastidon. We walked a short way along the road before reaching the start of the trail that led into the trees. The trail quickly began a series of zigzags to take us round a rocky bluff, crossing the dried up bed of a stream where in wetter times a waterfall would cascade down the steep cliffs above. There was now no trace of water, the water-smoothed rocks bone dry and earth collected in the rounded pot holes baked dry by the long summer sun.

A half hour of walking brought us to a narrow ledge where once again wire ropes and metal hand rails had been fixed into the rock face, providing comfort and reassurance for the precipitous walk high above the river. We were looking down, not just onto the distant river but the tops of trees as we negotiated the rocky ledge that in places was little more than six inches wide. High above our heads the vertical rock stretched skywards, beyond it a clear blue sky with the fading half-moon still visible and silhouettes of vultures soaring across the canyon.

The cool morning was warming up and I quickly shed my jumper, stuffing it into the rucksack and taking a long drink of water at the same time. Mike followed suit, opening his rucksack to a cloud of fromage that made the eyes water.

We met no one on that quiet stretch of canyon, no families, no noisy groups, no fit soldiers. It seemed all too soon before we climbed a short distance through the trees and reached the road at a sharp hairpin bend. Our last walk in the Verdon Gorge had come to an end. We emerged into a litter strewn layby on a sharp bend of the Moustier to Palud road. No cars were parked, the only people were a father and son on mountain bikes pausing for a drink in the shade of the trees. This layby was only a short distance from the layby from which we had embarked on the Sentier des Pecheurs earlier in the week and the two footpaths themselves were even closer together. Unfortunately the nature of the terrain in the gorge meant the two paths were not linked. Had they been, they would have formed part of a route linking with the Sentier Blanc Martel that would run for most of the length of the Verdon Gorge on its northern side. Maybe in years to come this link would be created and, if further work was undertaken at the far western end of the gorge, then it would be possible for walkers to complete the entire gorge on a single unbroken path.

We followed the road almost due north from its hairpin bend until the next hairpin bend, where a footpath left the road climbing through the trees and up through a narrow cleft at Ravin du Brusc. It was a steep climb from where we had left the road at 854 metres until the trees began to thin out and our path crossed the GR4 at over 1200 metres. At first the wood had been quite dense, deciduous oak mainly, but near the junction with the GR4 the woodland turned to pine trees, growing further apart, their shed cones and some branches crunching underfoot as we emerged into the sunshine. We were enveloped in the smell of sun-warmed pine. Wood ants were much in evidence in the thin dry soil, their nests often forming large conical domes made up of thousands of pine needles and thin twigs.

It was at the junction of the two paths that we met the first walkers of the day, an elderly couple and their big shaggy dog, walking slowly out of the trees from nowhere in particular.

"I don't know where they came from," said Mike, looking at the map. "But there's no footpath straight ahead. We turn right here."

So that's what we did, following a forest track. Large tyre marks indicated it was used for either logging or farming, but not on the large scales we have often seen at home. The trees became denser for a while and the temperature in the shade seemed more in keeping with the kind of October temperatures we were used to in England. A picnic bench was sitting in the shade, a convenient place for lunch although we would have preferred some sunshine. We stopped, putting on jumpers to offset the chilly shade. Another suitable picnic spot in the sun may be some way off, plus the thoughts of sitting on the ground or a fallen, rotting log with the possibility of numerous wood ants running about, was a little off putting! It's debatable whether the odour of Mike's cheese baguette would have attracted or repelled the ants. It was repelling me.

"Oh, delicious," mumbled Mike, taking a huge bite of baguette that oozed cheese.

"Hm, smells like it," I replied sarcastically, trying to judge if I was sitting up or down wind of him. Unfortunately there was no wind and the general miasma of rich, ripe French fromage filled the area around which we sat.

The woodland path continued, following the route of the GR4 for some distance all the way to Palud. At first the woodland was quite dense but soon we entered a large glade where coniferous trees were widely spaced, long grasses and wild flowers grew in the light areas of the woodland floor. Yellow leaved birch in their autumn colours contrasted with the dark green needles of the pines. A notice on one of the trees explained with the use of pictograms, and in French and English, that flocks were being guarded by dogs in this area. If we encountered such a flock we were to leave them in peace and to ignore the dog which, apparently, may come to investigate us and then return to guarding the flock. We had seen from a distance one such flock when on the walk up Le Chiran, and had pondered why a large, shaggy white dog was with the flock when there was seemingly no farmer present. This explained it. The notice went on to inform us that the dogs were specially trained and widely used in Haute Provence to guard against wolves and large cats.

Provence is home to many larger mammals including chamois, ibex and wild boar; but all the information I have been able to find about large felines suggests that the European lynx is found further north and east in the higher Alps. However, a cute looking small cat-like creature, the genet, is the closest thing to a big cat inhabiting the region of Haute Provence, and the genet is hardly big or ferocious enough to carry off a chicken never mind a sheep or a goat. One interesting contemporary article I did find was the ubiquitous 'big cat' sighting which seems to appear every so often in British newspapers: the Beast of Bodmin, the Fen Tiger, the Surrey Puma, the Kellas Cat and the Twickenham tabby, okay I might have made that last one up, but the others are all genuine claims of British sightings. Someone, or several someones it transpired, had reported seeing a large cat, possibly a black panther, roaming the hills and woods of Haute Provence, although the exact location was being withheld. Paw prints had been discovered that seemed to back up these claims and efforts were being made to catch the kitty but hunters had been asked not to shoot it. The article failed to say what these efforts were but Mike and I agreed that if we came across a big cat carrier with a saucer of milk inside we were ready to run.

I continued the remainder of the walk looking for flocks, dogs, wolves and large cats. I didn't see any. What I did see were a lot more ants, some very ugly looking crickets, numerous grasshoppers and a young couple straight out of an outdoor gear meets high end fashion catalogue. We heard the couple chatting before a bend in the path revealed them walking towards us a little way ahead. Tall, beautiful, young, blond and with perfect walking gear of clean boots, smart T-shirts, snug fitting shorts and tidy rucksacks, with hair fashionably held in place under neatly tied bandannas, they were everything we weren't. We plodded up hill, shorter, average looking, middle aged and greying, with hair doing its finest 'dragged through a hedge in every dimension' impression, dusty boots, trousers muddy at the knees, Mike with grease marks of melted fromage down his T-shirt, and me with my rucksack splattered with dried mud and what might have been a bit of sheep poo sticking to the back of it. They smiled and exchange happy hellos with us. We saw them again later in the afternoon, having obviously completed the same walk as us but in the opposite direction. By that time we were looking a bit dustier and I was looking decidedly sweatier. They still looked as fresh as a couple of cat walk models. I decided it must be my age.

The path began a descent through the trees, the bed of the track changing from compacted earth to loose gravel and dust. Not my favourite walking surface. As the trees began to thin and the path descend we came upon numerous trees that were hosts to large verdant balls of mistletoe. Mistletoe is a parasite and prefers certain species of tree on which to grow. The climate and the trees were proving ideal and great bundles of mistletoe grew in every tree.

"Ah, ah!" grinned Mike, wiggling his eyebrows and dragging me under a hanging bunch.

"Get off you silly sod! It's not Christmas yet," I protested half-heartedly.

He ignored me. A situation I have long grown accustomed to. We continued down the path, Mike on the lookout for more overhead excuses, me contemplating the traditions of Christmas and vegetation.

"It's odd when you think about it," I began.

"What is? Kissing?"

"No... Get off! This tradition of bringing green plants into the house at Christmas. Especially when

164

you consider most of them are poisonous: mistletoe, ivy, holly, Brussels sprouts…"

My knees were protesting with every downhill step by the time the track turned into a metalled surface and we reachcd a lovely house that marked the outskirts of Palud. It was mid-afternoon and the village was asleep again, assuming it had ever woken up since the last time we were there. An old woman was sweeping in front of her house and a grumpy dog set up a monotonous barking at us as we passed. The woman shouted something, the dog ignored her, so she shouted something else and it still ignored it.

"Quiet!" Mike tried in English. The dog shut up.

Across the main road we followed a narrow lane that ran between fields before reaching a dried up stream, we turned left, got lost, consulted the map, commented on the lack of footpath signs just when you needed them, and eventually picked out the correct route. Soon we were back on the road leading to the car, the sides of the ravine were closing in and we found ourselves walking in a suddenly much cooler shadowy spot that had not seen the sun all day. At a bend in the road, where signs warned of icy patches, several minibuses were parked (not that one) and we could hear people calling to one another as they climbed the nearby crags in the Ravin de Mainmorte.

It was a relief to reach the car and be able to get our walking boots off, standing in bare feet on the gravel surface, enjoying the cool air to our sweaty toes. I thought I caught another whiff of Mike's sandwiches but he assured me kindly that it was probably my socks, I assured him equally kindly that, mistletoe or no mistletoe, Christmas was cancelled.

€-€-€-€-€

The larger supermarket on the edge of Moustiers was closed once again, despite notices to the contrary. We drove on, keeping a close lookout for dogs crossing the road and parked in the car park close to the cemetery. Dumping rucksacks and dusty walking boots in the apartment we hurried out to see if the new, smaller supermarket just down the narrow alley from our apartment was open. Mike was overjoyed to find that it was and hurried straight to the wine section. The shop had a small footprint, and a good heel's-worth of it was given over to alcohol. But this wasn't your usual selection of numerous multi-can packs of cheap lager, there were a few varieties of lager and continental beer but, as you might expect, this tiny French supermarket stocked mainly wine, much of which was locally produced. Not something you can say about English supermarkets! Whilst I admired the fresh locally produced garlic, beans and salad crops, Mike gazed with longing and some confusion at the cornucopia of wines on display.

"Oh, just pick one!" I impatiently exclaimed, my knowledge and liking for alcohol running to Bailey's and the odd glass of Pimms.

166

"There's so much choice," sighed Mike.

"There! That one has a nice label, a pretty picture of a chateau," I pointed. "And it's cheap."

"You don't go off the label and the price," replied Mike, rolling his eyes.

"You weren't saying that the other day when you were quaffing your €3 bottle of plonk!"

"Okay, fair point," he conceded.

Whilst he dithered over which of the many reds to purchase, I surreptitiously added a packet of chocolate biscuits to the basket. I could have added half the shop in the time it was taking him to pick a bottle and he would have remained oblivious! Finally he opted for a bottle of Cab Sav (whatever that is!) and we paid a grand total of €3.70, most of which was accounted for by the biscuits.

We returned to the apartment with a plan in mind. Grabbing a wine glass and corkscrew we hurried up a nearby alley and out along the ramparts to Mike's seat, as he referred to it, located just by the bend in the track near the dried up cascade. Mike's seat was taken by some tourists – how dare they! He hurried on muttering to himself, to the next seat which was empty, thank goodness, I don't think I could have borne him otherwise. He was starting to behaviour as if he had a drink problem. We settled down in the sunshine on the perforated metal bench, which was actually more comfortable than it sounded, Mike opened the wine and I opened the biscuits.

"When did you get those?" he asked, noticing them for the first time.

"While you were doing your Oz Clarke," I sighed. "Or should that be Jilly Goolden?"

Mike declared the wine most satisfying. I thought the same about the biscuits. A few people strolled past, smiling in amusement when they saw us. The afternoon sun was starting to lose some of its heat and the moon was already starting to appear behind the rocky ravine. Birds sang out of sight in the olive grove and I was just craning my neck to try to see them when one suddenly flew into the branches above our heads. We had seen a lot of birds in Provence from the huge vultures to the tiny gold crests and many in between, mainly blackbirds, robins and great tits. But this distinctive little bird was one I had never seen before, although they do live in Britain.

"Ooh!" I squeaked with excitement, trying to be quiet and not frighten it away. "It's a crested tit."

"Where?" whispered Mike, leaning forward and nearly spilling his wine.

Crested tits are the same size as blue tits and as the name suggests have crests on their heads but lack any blue feathers. With pale brown upper parts, rather off white underneath and neatly marked black and white faces, they would be rather undistinguished were it not for the triangular crest of feathers on the top of their heads. These clever little birds have an omnivorous diet consisting of insects and seeds, and store food in winter. We watched the tit as it hopped between the branches and twigs above our heads for a few minutes before finally flying off amongst the olive trees.

"I've seen crested tits in Scotland," remarked Mike.

Scotland and specifically the Caledonian pine forest is the only place in Britain you are likely to see this characterful little bird. In continental Europe their range is much greater, excluding only higher latitudes of Scandinavia, and Italy and parts of south eastern Europe.

The crested tit, half the bottle of wine and most of the biscuits were gone (how did that happen?), the sun was rapidly going too and so as the day began to cool we collected our belongings and returned to the apartment. Mike uploaded a photograph onto his Facebook page, it soon earned several posts as friends viewed the image of him sitting on a bench clutching a wine glass and a bottle of red wine.

"All he needs is a paper bag!" commented one friend much to my amusement.

We had one more day to go in Provence and with the trails in the Verdon Gorge completed we searched the maps and guide books for another good walk. One option was to travel some distance back towards Castellane, to walk amongst the woods and mountains near the tiny village of Chasteuil. But it would be a long drive and with a long and early drive back to Nice the day after we decided to stay closer to Moustiers.

The cheese had finally been eaten, I could say 'run out' but from the smell it had been threatening to do that for some time! We took a packed lunch of chorizo and baguettes, chocolate and apples and headed west from Moustiers towards the village of Sainte Jurs.

"Where we need to go is not on any of my maps," said Mike worryingly as we left the village.

"So how do you know where we're going?" I asked.

"The walk is on this map," he said, flapping a local tourist map about. "But before we get to Sainte Jurs, which is also on this map, we leave the road map and there's a little bit of erm, guess work, to link up the two maps."

"So, just to get this right, we're driving off one map, into a map-less void of unknown terrain and turnings, and hopefully then driving back onto another map."

"Yes, but I'm sure we'll be fine. We need to turn off the main road somewhere on top of the plateau."

"Navigating by the sun are you?" I asked wryly, as we drove out of the trees and crested the top of the plateau, the fields stretching before us and a couple of side turnings bearing down on us rather quickly.

My sarcastic comment referred to a disastrous drive through the streets of a French city on a previous holiday where we had become utterly lost and rather out of sorts with one another. And apparently, reminding him of it had touched a raw nerve. As we drove closer to a couple of turnoffs Mike waved his hand vaguely and barked something that sounded like a particularly unpleasant four letter word beginning with 't'. A word that, in fairness, he has never called me before.

"Which way?" I demanded as the turnings got ever nearer. "It's no good swearing and waving your hand about when I'm not looking!"

His response this time was to call me the same name again, accompanied with a jab of his hand to indicate the turning on the right.

"Will you stop calling me that!" I snapped, slamming the brakes on, dropping a couple of gears and turning right onto the side road. (Who would have thought a Renault Twingo could wheel spin)?

"What? I've not called you anything!" protested Mike.

"You just called me a twat!"

"I didn't!"

"Yes you did!"

"No I didn't! I told you to turn right."

"You waved your hand vaguely to the right and called me a twat!"

"Oh god," Mike rolled his eyes. "I said: 'droite'."

"What? That sounds like something else to me!"

"Droite. Pronounced drwaht. Spelt D R O I T E."

"Oh, like adroite! As in adept, skilful, competent?"

"Something you're certainly not when it comes to French," he sighed. "No, droite as in right, as in turn right, as in take a right turn, as in not left."

"Oh," I muttered. "So what's left?"

"Gauche."

"Oh! As in uncouth, inept, awkward…"

"If you say so."

"So what's straight on?"

"Do you really want to know?" he sighed.

"Yes, I might need to know this."

"Tout droit."

"Too?"

"Tout."

"I thought tout meant all, as in 'is that all?' if you are buying croissants or something." I was beginning to get confused. "I'm beginning to get confused."

"I'm beginning to get a headache. Tout does mean 'all' but in this case it also means straight on," he said with more patience than I probably warranted by now.

"Anyway, there's a junction coming up," I interrupted. "Which way now?"

"Right."

"Thank you."

We were nearly off the map, travelling up a rather bumpy, narrow road that had patches of weeds growing in the middle. I was beginning to doubt Mike's navigational skills but he assured me there would soon be a left turn that would lead to Sainte Jurs. The road climbed steadily and the hills above Moustiers Sainte-Marie soon came into view. The only thing not coming into view was a turn off to the left. After a couple of miles, Mike admitted we had gone too far and must have missed a turn off. I turned the car around and we retraced our route. He was correct we had missed a turn off but only because the turn off in question was a gravel track that in Britain would have passed for a forest trail or a bridle way.

"Well, we can't drive down there," I commented.

"No, we'll have to go back to the plateau and take the longer route."

So that is what we did, joining the road on the plateau and following it as it weaved through a couple of large villages, turning droite once or twice until we finally saw a road sign pointing to Sainte Jurs. This road took us in a straight line, through lavender fields that in places were still in flower, giving us a small idea of the rich purple that would clothe the whole of the plateau in the height of summer. At the entrance to Sainte Jurs we reached a vague junction, the village itself seems to sit at the end of the road and no signs were in evidence to help Mike navigate to our final destination just beyond the village.

Sainte Jurs is another perched village. Narrow streets, a few houses, a small square and a little car park. It had all the appearance of yet another sleepy village of Haute Provence and with a population of eighty it was hardly Nice. But that had not always been the case. In the nineteenth century it had been a thriving industrial community, hard though it was to believe today. The population peaked at 535 in 1836 and at its most productive the village had five gypsum mines. Gypsum is used for plaster making, and the gypsum of Saint Jurs was the largest export of the region. Today there is still sufficient gypsum left to liberally coat any vehicle, as we were soon to discover. A village had existed here long before the dusty gypsum mines, as early as the twelfth century a chapel was erected, dedicated to Sainte Georges. It was destroyed in 1793 and has since undergone considerable restoration, the latest restoration occurring in the 1980s after the priest put his foot down and refused to conduct any more funerals there because the building had become so dangerous – possibly he feared he ran the risk of creating more work for himself! The restored chapel remains but the sixteenth century castle is now in ruins, no priest to stick up for it presumably.

We drove into the village, squeezing through the narrow streets in the hope we were heading in the right direction. Turns out we were heading straight for a camper van. A big camper van. A big camper van on a narrow twisty street, with no possibility of it reversing. I stopped the car and opened the door. Wrong hand. I closed the door, eliciting a querulous raised eyebrow from Mike. Did he think I was baling out?

"Wrong hand," I explained before putting the gear lever into reverse and carefully driving backwards until I reached a narrow opening that I could pull into to allow the camper van past.

The Dutch couple inside the camper waved and smiled and squeezed their way out of the village. I put the car in first gear and set off again. A tractor appeared. Well, it made a change from a camper van. No reversing for me this time though! I accelerated hard, aiming for the entrance to the car park, reaching it just before the tractor and slipped in (adroitly I might say) before the farmer could force me to reverse.

"Okay, where now?" I asked, feeling very pleased to have beaten the tractor.

"Back the way we came," replied Mike, bending over one of the maps.

"What?"

"I think we need to skirt the village, not go through it."

"Now you tell me."

We squeezed back out of the village and turned immediately right, along a narrow lane that soon began to climb around the back of the village and into the forest.

"This is more like it!" proclaimed Mike.

But I was having my doubts. The tarmac ran out, to be replaced with dusty, rutted gravel. If I had balked at driving down the forest track a short while earlier, this seemed even worse. The track continued and so did we, with Mike assuring me we were going the right way, and me doubting his every word with each new bend in the track and rut in the road. I was forced to swerve from one side of the track to the other to avoid the increasing number of drainage channels and pot holes. (Who would have thought a Renault Twingo could go rallying)?

"Are you absolutely sure about this?" I demanded, as I slowed to a crawl to cross an exhaust-threatening rut, thinking of our €700 insurance excess.

"Yes, just keep going. Good driving by the way."

"Droite!" I muttered in my best French accent.

What felt like several days later we reached a bend where the track widened to find five cars parked at the side of the track. Had it not been for that I would have probably refused to drive any further, but seeing those cars gave me some reassurance that Mike was right (not that I was inclined to admit that to him at the time) and I continued, as directed, up the track.

"There should be another car park in a couple of hundred yards," he gasped as the car gave a particularly big lurch into an unseen pot hole.

Clouds of dust rose up in the rear view mirror as the track continued to climb and we continued to bounce around in the little car. The views through the trees into the valley on our left were probably quite good, but all I could see out of the side and rear windows was a grey patina of dust. The windscreen I kept having to clear with the wipers and plenty of screen wash, oops wrong stalk! That was the horn!

At another bend we finally emerged from the trees where a grassy green sward was already filling with cars. Mike looked smug as he directed me onto the grass. Several people were milling around the cars, possibly the French equivalent of the Ramblers. A walking group obviously, but thankfully no white minibus! The car creaked and groaned as we climbed out and surveyed the body work. No marks were visible, actually no bodywork was visible, there was just a Twingo-shaped grey dusty thing sitting there.

"Glad our insurance excess excludes returning a filthy car," laughed Mike.

We took our time with rucksacks and boots, allowing the Ramblers to get ahead of us. The first part of the walk followed the track; pretty soon our boots and lower legs matched the car. After more than a kilometre along the track we reached another parking area, at which point Mike declared it was this car park he thought we had parked at! The droite! Although in truth, I'm not sure whether I would have preferred to walk or drive to it. The track had been dusty and not particularly interesting as is often the case with forest tracks.

Shortly afterwards we turned off, heading into the trees, mainly coniferous, and climbing up through the sun dappled pines before emerging onto a steep open grassy slope that led to the summit of Montdenier at 1751 metres. The mountain is, apparently, a favourite of paragliders, but our guidebook warned (in case we had managed to squeeze a paragliding kit into our suitcase – fat chance with all those teabags) that take-offs can be turbulent if a north wind is blowing. Any take-off would be turbulent in my case!

Before reaching the summit we walked along the ridge, a mixture of short grass, thyme and juniper bushes with, in small patches, the rich blue flowers of delicate gentians growing close to the ground. To the left the land fell away sharply into a wooded valley where brilliant reds and oranges of deciduous trees threw colourful splashes amongst the dark green bows of the conifers. Beyond the far side of the valley the mountains rose up in a series of ridges, stretching away to the Alps. Extending far below to the west was the Valensole Plateau, the major lavender growing region of Provence, sitting 500 metres above sea level it covers an area of eight thousand square kilometres. The town of Valensole sits in a braided river valley and this wide valley was clearly visible from where we were standing. Shifting channels that constantly deposit and wash away sediments and gravel create many shallow water courses that are forever changing creating a river that has the appearance of a braid, hence the name. Valensole was one of several places we simply did not have time to visit, which was a shame as apart from being another historical town it also boasts over three hundred days of sunshine a year. Burnley's very similar.

The sun was hot by the time we stopped for lunch further along the ridge. We found a couple of flat rocks overlooking the valley and shrugged out of our rucksacks, grateful for the rest and the crusty baguettes. Stretching ahead of us, the ridge threw up a series of jagged rocky edges where the limestone beds had been turned into an upright position by earth movements millions of years ago. Over time some of the layers had been opened up by weathering and by determined plant roots finding their way down into the cracks. In the valley bottom many of the trees had been cleared to provide enclosed fields and in one we could see, through binoculars, a flock of sheep being guarded by a large dog. It was possible to pick out a narrow ribbon of road running part way up the opposite side of the valley; and dotted along the road were occasional farms and a cluster of houses.

My rucksack so admired the valley it attempted to fall into it. As I was reaching for it to put away the sandwich wrappings, it slipped out of my grasping fingers and, weighted with water in my platypus, began tobogganing down the grassy slope. I managed to grab it within feet of the sheer cliff edge but I gave Mike an anxious few seconds when he thought I was going over the edge with the car keys.

A distinctive call had us both swivelling our necks and looking skywards, we had heard the sound of Alpine choughs. Very similar but a different species to the choughs found in parts of Cornwall, Scotland and Wales, the Alpine chough has a slightly different voice and, instead of the red bill and legs of our British birds, has red legs and a yellow bill. It is common to see them in groups but as we sat atop Montdenier we could only see two of these acrobatic and colourful birds. In summer the Alpine choughs feed on insects but in the harsher, colder winters their diet is mainly seeds and berries; opportunistic, they will take food scraps at any time of year from the high mountain ski resorts and we had seen many in past holidays doing just that around restaurant terraces and mountain tops in the Alps and Pyrenees.

We followed the ridge back to the steep slope and began a knee cracking descent as the group we had seen earlier in the day began their ascent. Where they had been in the intervening time we were unsure, but with so many trails in the area it was likely they had picked a different route to ours. At the bottom of the slope we took a twisting path off to our left that climbed once more into trees to reach a lower hilltop marked on the map as Vigie. More sensational views and an orientation table greeted us at the summit. We sat enjoying the views and a bar of chocolate that was quickly melting in the warm sun.

A different path led us down Vigie, sharp bends between trees and more open shrubby slopes taking us gradually down the hillside on a zigzag route back towards the car. We seemed to be descending a long way but were distracted firstly by the views and secondly by a bit of insect natural history. We had seen praying mantises individually on several occasions that week, but this was the first time we saw two together. Although by the time we saw them it was more one and three quarters than two. I had heard that after mating the female praying mantis eats her mate, some authorities poo poo this idea but the

BBC Wildlife website stated it as fact and seeing is believing after all. We had missed the sex bit, well, it would have been a bit voyeuristic to watch that, but we were just in time for the post coital snack. And don't all wildlife programmes consist of animals either eating one another or mating? With praying mantises you get both! The female had already eaten her mate's head, not that this had stopped him from moving about, two legs continued to wave as if in protest but she doggedly ignored him and carried on munching down into his thorax, steadily working her way along his body. The only time she stopped eating was when Mike got a little too close with the camera, at which point she picked up her half mate and, waving a warning leg or three at Mike, shuffled away from him before continuing to eat. Okay, so that's nature for you. Cruel? Brutal? Lacking in romance? Perhaps; but then we have our traditions: post coital cup of tea if you're lucky, turning over, farting and snoring if you're not; and praying mantises have theirs: eating their mate. Actually, put like that, ours don't seem so bad now!

Mike was beginning to empathise a little too much with what was left of the leg-waving male mantis and so we resumed our walk back to the car. The track stopped zigzagging long enough to take us back into the denser coniferous woodland before emerging suddenly onto the dusty track that passed for a road in these parts. My knees were beginning to ache from the constant downhills as we turned left for more downhill but this time with added dust. After fifteen minutes of walking the car was still nowhere in sight.

182

But Mike was generally an excellent map reader and I trudged along behind him daydreaming about pain au chocolat. I looked up with a start on hearing Mike's muttered curse.

"What's up?"

But I hardly needed an answer. We had reached a car park. Unfortunately it was the wrong car park. Even more unfortunately it was one of the car parks we had driven past on our way up the mountain that morning.

"This map's not very good," excused Mike, waving the tourist map that we had been relying on that day.

I could hardly blame him as even I could see he was correct. That day's walk had not been covered by our 1 : 25 000 Carte Topographique, instead we had been using a free map issued by the tourist office and although the scale was the same the detail and quality were a lot worse. We are spoilt in Britain with the finest mapping in the world, nothing else matches Ordnance Survey for detail and clarity, even I can navigate with an O.S. map! (Mike might dispute that). Not only is there less detail on non O.S. maps but the text is miniscule, and nowhere will you find a symbol for a pub! Although I do think the Ordnance Survey could improve their maps ever so slightly by the introduction of a symbol for cake shops.

So having seen some cars that weren't ours and muttered over the mapping, we turned round and trudged back up the dusty track. Sometime later we

reached the right car park, where a dusty grey hump
of metal sat waiting for us.

€-€-€-€-€

It was a sad and dusty drive back to Moustiers, sad
because this was our last day, dusty because every
time we opened the windows clouds of grey dust
swept in from the body work. The crescent moon
was peeking over the ravine above the village as we
descended from the plateau and drove down the
valley and then up the steep road into the village.

A pot of tea and a biscuit, a shower and then we set
about packing everything we wouldn't be wearing the
next day. With the packing completed we set about
cleaning the apartment. Madame was due to call that
evening to inspect everything and (hopefully) return
our security deposit, and we were keen to give her no
excuse not to do so. I was just reaching for a broom
and a mop when there was a knock at the door.
Madame was early!

I opened the door, clutching a sweeping brush, with
the garbled greeting of: "Er, bonjour. We were just
about to clean!"

"Bonsoir," she replied breezing in and spinning
round, seeming to take in everything at once.
Suppose she wanted to inspect the bathroom? Mike
hadn't started to clean it yet and there was toothpaste
on the taps! And the floor was covered in dusty
footprints from Sainte Jurs!

"Bonsoir," replied Mike calmly, standing there in a pair of fetching yellow gloves and clutching a bottle of Cif. (All he needed to complete the ensemble was an apron).

"You have had a good holiday, oui?" Madame asked with a smile.

"Aye, yes, er, oui," I replied, running through a repertoire of broad Burnley, English and terrible French.

Mike rolled his eyes, (I think Madame might have done too) and they began chatting about the unseasonably dry weather we had been fortunate to have.

"Tomorrow it rains, all next week it rains," Madame informed us.

"We're leaving at the right time then," I said. Knowing the weather was due to change softened the thought of going home.

"So, how is zee coffee machine?"

"Good," replied Mike

"And zee television?" she asked, looking at it as if inspecting for damage, which she probably was.

"Same rubbish as at home but a different language," I replied before I could stop myself.

"It's fine, good, yes," Mike assured Madame.

Seemingly satisfied that we hadn't trashed the apartment, and trusting us to clean the dusty footprints off the floor, she happily refunded us our deposit. Biding us a safe journey home she left, breezing out as she had breezed in and nearly tripping over the mop that I had left in the doorway.

We cleaned and then cooked a final meal of pasta. Then, wrapping up in coats, hat and gloves, we took the camera and went for a last evening stroll around the village. The moon was high in the sky, an owl hooted somewhere in the olive groves and a solitary cat slunk between doorways as we made our way up towards the chapel to take in the clear night sky. Headlights of a few cars picked out the line of the road leading up onto the plateau opposite. We took a last stroll down from the chapel, slipping once again on the smoothly polished stones of the path, and descended into the village to walk the narrow lanes one final time. I get very maudlin on the last evening of a holiday, I'm not sure how Mike stands it sometimes, but he just humours me and allows himself to be dragged along.

We had an early start the next morning. Our flight departed mid-morning and with a two hour check-in time and having to return the hire car, plus an unknown drive of possibly two hours, we were up long before the sun or anyone else in Moustiers Sainte-Marie. A quick breakfast, a final tidy up and we stumbled, suitcase in hand, down the narrow stairs, out of the apartment and through the sleeping village.

Our drive from Nice to Moustiers on our first day had been along the scenic routes but it had taken several hours. Our drive back to Nice would hopefully take considerably less time as we were following a more direct route, on a faster, better road that would lead us to the autoroute and eventually to Nice. For the first hour the roads were almost empty, we drove through the pre-dawn darkness with the headlights cutting a swathe of illumination onto the wood-bordered road. At Aups, Mike and a plethora of road signs directed me through the narrow streets, empty squares and past old stone buildings. Approaching the larger Draguignan we almost got lost, road signs contradicting the map Mike was carefully studying. I was happy to drive, taking direction that turned out to be accurate. Soon we were on a busy dual carriageway, surrounded by heavy traffic and numerous buses taking early morning commuters into the town. The dark was now cut through with light as bill boards, street signs, vehicles and buildings were lit up against the darkness of early morning. Beyond Draguignan we soon reached the first of three toll booths that marked the busier highways and autoroutes.

"Go to that booth!" instructed Mike, pointing to one lit up with a huge green Euro symbol. "The others might only take credit card or token."

We drew up behind a couple of cars and took our turn to throw handfuls of coins into the gaping mouth of the automated payment machine. It spat out some change said something I didn't understand but which Mike assured me was 'thank you' in both French and English, the light changed to green and we were away. Eight huge lanes of traffic converging into three as the toll booths were left behind. Dawn slowly arrived, lightening the sky almost imperceptibly at first. By the time we had negotiated our third toll booth we were heading north east, passing exits for Cannes and Antibes as we drew ever closer to Nice. This was now rush hour traffic, snarling bumper to bumper at times as vehicles exited and new ones joined the busy autoroute. I was concentrating on quatre-vingts things at once and Mike was busy watching out for our exit slip road. The time was already eight o'clock, leaving us not much time to get to the airport. We need not have worried, we hit the slip road to find traffic in Nice not as bad as we had been expecting.

Next stop was a petrol station, the hire agreement specified we had to return the car full of fuel. This was only the second time we had filled the car, Mike operating the pump whilst I went in to pay, a simple task concluded with a minimum of communication, as we were the only customers I did not even have to tell the cashier the pump number. A smile, a bonjour, a handful of Euros and a merci and I was on my way back to the car.

With just a mile to go to the car drop off point and a full tank of petrol we hit a traffic jam. Ten minutes of inching forward finally brought us in sight of the hotel from which we had hired the car. We were nearly there! And then fate intervened in the form of road works which had not been there when we picked the car up. We needed to turn right and drive clockwise around the hotel to reach the entrance to the underground car park. That's what we needed to do. And that's just what we couldn't do. The traffic management now installed would not allow us to turn right. I would need to go straight on at the temporary traffic lights and then do a U-turn in the middle of four lanes of traffic if I wanted to be able to drive round the hotel. Confused? Yes, so was Mike, up until that moment his navigation had been faultless, but suddenly it deserted him. But I, for once, was not confused. Sitting at the head of the queue waiting for the temporary traffic lights to change to green, I had been carefully watching the oncoming cars and I knew just what needed to be done. The only thing was I wasn't sure if there was a central kerb in the middle of the road that might try to stop me! As the lights changed to green and Mike was still muttering something along the lines of 'oh god, we can't turn right' (not much help at that moment) I accelerated away (who would have thought a Renault Twingo could leave skid marks?) pulled ahead of the car next to me and then flicked the indicator onto left, pulling the wheel across and executing a tight U-turn that resulted in us joining the end of the queue of traffic facing back the way we had just come.

"Eeek! What the?" squealed Mike, grabbing for the dashboard.

Goodness knows what his reaction would have been if there had been a kerb, for I had already decided I was going to drive over it should the need have arisen!

"It's fine," I calmly reassured, as the lights changed to green and I set off, driving around the side of the hotel and taking the turn into the underground car park.

A young woman was waiting to take collection of the car and waved me into the narrow parking space by the little rental kiosk. I got out, leaving Mike to make sure we had emptied the car. The young woman smiled and said something in French. Oh, no here we go. I smiled back, wracking my brains for the French for 'sorry I'm an English idiot and don't understand a word you're saying'. Fortunately Mike clambered out of the car at that moment, so I pointed to him. Surely he would understand? Actually, no, he didn't. The young woman tried again, this time speaking more slowly and a little louder. We offered her every bit of paper we had relating to the hire car. She shook her head at all of them and tried again. We still didn't understand. Eventually we all realised we were getting nowhere and by mutual agreement and much smiling gave up.

"I thought you could speak French better than me," I remarked as we made our way up the stairs to the hotel reception.

"The cat speaks French better than you!" he laughed. "My French isn't that good. I think it's all relative."

Emerging into reception we had one last thing to do before we went to the airport. On picking up the car I had left a security deposit using my credit card. I wanted to make sure that it would be refunded. The man who had attended to us when we hired the car was not there and the desk was empty, so we made our way over to the main reception desk. Two members of staff were standing behind the counter, one was talking to a guest and the other, a smartly dressed woman, was shuffling some papers.

I approached the woman, last chance to get my French correct. I had no chance of asking for a refund on my credit card in French but at least I could manage to ask her in French if she spoke English. Make an effort at least, I told myself as I cleared my throat and in what I thought was reasonable French asked the question. There was a pause and the hotel lobby fell silent as everyone turned to stare at me. The woman looked at me, rather quizzically I thought, and I began to rapidly review in my mind what I had just said to her, I had a dim idea in the back of my mind that I hadn't quite got it right! And then it came to me with an embarrassingly sickening lurch.

"Do you mean English?" she asked with some confusion.

She might well have been confused. I had just asked her, in French, if she spoke French.

"You've done it again!" exclaimed Mike, rolling his eyes and dissolving into fits of laughter.

He wasn't the only one. The woman was laughing, the guest was laughing and the other receptionist was laughing. And yes, I too was laughing. I must have made their day. Mike's been dining out on it ever since. So you see it's true what they say, if you make an effort it's always appreciated, even if only for its comedic value.

Fin.

Information:

Provence and particularly the region around the Verdon Gorge is beautiful at any time of year. We visited in autumn when colours of the trees and foliage are at their best.

The climate in Provence is generally dry and hot in summer, with warm springs and mild autumns, although the temperatures drop often to freezing at night during autumn. Autumn and winter are generally the wettest times of year with October being the wettest month, which makes our rain-free week something of a rarity.

In the summer months and the high season, whilst all the facilities will be open, giving the visitor more options on where to stay and which activities to undertake, the roads, campsites, hotels, restaurants etc. will be very busy.

Most organised activities such as canyoning and white water rafting are only available during the spring and summer. Walking and rock climbing, and boating on Lac de Sainte-Croix are possible year round.

The high season gets extremely busy and advanced booking of campsites, hotels and other accommodation is recommended.

Camping is by far the cheapest form of accommodation and there are dozens of campsites in the area offering a range of facilities – but no toilet paper!

The main bases for accommodation and activity companies are Castellane, Moustiers Sainte-Marie and Palud; with smaller villages around Lac de Sainte-Croix also offering plenty of choice.

Internet searches of Verdon Gorge, Moustiers Sainte-Marie, Castellane and Haute Provence will bring up pages of websites, some for private companies, some for accommodation providers and some for the official sites of towns and villages from which is it possible to find links to accommodation and activities in those places. We booked our rental apartment via the Moustiers Sainte-Marie website.

All except the smallest villages will have a shop of some description. But remember, opening hours are restricted and most will close on Sundays and for one or two hours at midday. There are supermarkets at Grasse, Castellane, Riez and Aup as well as many other larger villages and towns.

Various airlines travel to Nice, the nearest airport. Whilst not a huge airport it is served by several car rental companies, and it is always worth searching online for best flight and car hire prices.

For most walks in the region good walking boots are essential. As we found, even the paths around the villages can be rough and stony. In autumn and spring early morning temperatures can be quite cool, and when the sun starts to set the temperatures can drop rapidly, so it is wise to take plenty of layers of clothing.

Driving on French roads – well I could write a book. Most guide books will give a brief run-down of the rules of the road. Just remember: drive on the right and change gear with the right hand. Before hiring a car don't be tempted to get the largest you can if there's only a couple of you. The mountain roads are often narrow, crash barriers are rare and there are numerous wide campervans lurking around every corner.

There are numerous guide books available on Provence and the Cote D'Azur, all providing a useful insight to the drives, walks, activities and places of interest. For the walks we purchased the 'Carte Topographique 3442 OT' which covers the area around the Verdon Gorge. Footpaths are generally well signposted with route names and distances, and different coloured lines, often placed on rocks and tree trunks, indicate the type of footpath.

An understanding of basic French is useful, although not vital, as most people do speak some English. However it's always nice to make the effort to speak the language, most people appreciate it. Plus it provides great entertainment when you get it wrong.

By the Same Author:

Cycling Across England
© Julia R May 2012
https://tinyurl.com/yc62pful

Two women, two bikes, no backup on a Sea to Sea adventure.

At the beginning of the twenty-first century two friends set off to cycle from coast to coast across England. For one, it was to be the first of many long distance cycle rides.

Cycling Across England is an account of the fun, the food, the mountains, the moorlands and the mathematics the two friends encountered along the way. From the Irish Sea, through the mountains of Cumbria and the Pennine uplands they travelled through a landscape of contrasts to finish their journey in the industrial northeast on the North Sea coast. Broken glass, slugs and arduous ascents were relieved by blackberries, an excess of pizza and delightful descents. Join them as they cycle across England on this iconic ride.

I've Cycled Through There
© Julia R May 2012
https://tinyurl.com/ybxf3gfj

That strangest of traveller, the lone female, is at it
again. This time cycling through the heart of England
from Bath to London to her home in Lancashire. For
such a small country England was proving to be a
land of contrasts and surprises; from the leafy lanes of
Berkshire to the bleak moorlands of the north,
spectacular scenery and post-industrial mill towns,
dead divas and murderous mad men.

Throughout the six hundred mile cycle ride there was
much that was quintessentially English: Georgian
architecture and thatched cottages, William
Shakespeare and Samuel Johnson, Bath buns and
Yorkshire pudding, canals and Roman roads, Magna
Carta and the Houses of Parliament, oh, and
Maharajah's Wells and teams of huskies!

Share the experience, the food, the fun and the
frustrations. Funny and factual by turns, this is a true
account of a cycle journey home through the heart of
England.

Walking with Hadrian
© Julia R May 2012
https://tinyurl.com/y9929ggz

A walk through time and fog along Hadrian's Wall.

Built almost two thousand years ago on the orders of
the Emperor Hadrian and marking the northern-most
boundary of the Roman Empire, Hadrian's Wall is
one of Britain's most enduring ancient monuments
and a UNESCO World Heritage Site. In 2003 a
footpath following the line of the Wall was
designated as a National Trail running 84 miles across
England from the Solway Firth to the North Sea.
Since then walkers have been coming to enjoy this
long distance path in the wild landscape of northern
England, and a few years later inadvertently choosing
the foggiest week she could, Julia finally got round to
walking the Wall.

Factual and funny by turns, 'Walking with Hadrian'
is an accurate account of the history, culture, scenery
and wildlife of Hadrian's Wall Path. Battling fog,
maps, social networking and the encroaching perils of
middle age, the author has added another book to her
collection of traveller's tales.

Cycles and Sandcastles
© Julia R May 2013
https://tinyurl.com/yba8rbqz

Running two hundred miles from Newcastle to Edinburgh, the Coast and Castles Cycle Route promised to be a journey through millennia of turbulent history and fabulous scenery.   It proved to be more than just ruined castles and wild coastline. More industrial heritage, more rain, more cross dressing stag nights, more stunning beaches, more wildlife, more grave robbers, more railways, more tea rooms and the Moorfoot Hills.

Close encounters with seagulls, precocious children, warrior-like toddlers and bathroom cleaning products were all in a day's cycling for the author as she pedalled north, passing remote beaches, wooded river valleys and more castles than you could shake a bicycle pump at.

Written with self-deprecating humour and a wry eye for detail, Cycles and Sandcastles is a narrative of the history, the scenery and the flavours of a bike ride through Northumberland and the Scottish Borders.

Bicycles, Boats and Bagpipes
© Julia R May 2014
https://tinyurl.com/y7hrnokp

Having cycled the length and breadth of the British mainland, it was time for a change. After seeing a little blue cycle route sign on the west coast of Scotland, Julia was struck with inspiration. The islands of the Outer Hebrides beckoned. There was just one problem, her boyfriend wanted to go too! Looking on the bright side he could be responsible for navigating and could take most of the luggage. Well, that was the plan. Little did she realise that with her boyfriend there also came his smelly footwear and holey cycling leggings.

Bicycles, Boats and Bagpipes is a detailed and often amusing account of a 500 mile cycle journey through the beautiful and remote islands of the Outer Hebrides and along the mountainous northwest coast of the Scottish mainland.

But it wasn't all about the cycling; there were the rare flower-rich machairs of the Western Isles, idyllic white sandy beaches, blue seas, wild moorland and ancient historic sites to explore. Wildlife to watch. Ferries to sail. Cake to eat and tea to drink. And throughout the trip the experience of isolated communities going about their daily lives, such a contrast from the hustle and bustle of home.

Bicycles, Beer and Black Forest Gateau
© Julia R May 2016
https://tinyurl.com/yctr5bbg

Not many people would consider cycling hundreds miles through Europe to be a relaxing holiday. Mike certainly didn't. But Julia did, she was peculiar that way. There was a challenge to be had in following the River Rhine from its source high in the Swiss Alps, through Germany, France and the Netherlands to the North Sea. But if Mike could not be convinced by mention of the varied scenery, the cultural diversity and the cake, what would change his mind? Finally it was mention of the hundreds of breweries in Germany that convinced him. Who knew, it might turn out to be very relaxing after all?

But as the couple were to discover, cycling on the continent can be very different to cycling in Britain. It was not just the language that would prove difficult to get to grips with, the rules of the road, the navigation, the continental heat and the alpine thunderstorms would test their patience as would tractor drivers and mosquitoes. But most challenging of all would be two weeks without a proper cup of tea. Would beer, gateaux and chocolate be enough to compensate?

Dawdling Through The Dales
© Julia R May 2018
https://tinyurl.com/y8kew292

The Dales Way long distance footpath runs for over
eighty miles from Ilkley to Bowness-on-Windermere,
encompassing the beautiful scenery of North
Yorkshire and Cumbria and two National Parks. It is
a varied walk of ever-changing scenery of lush river
valleys, limestone pavements, moorland and
mountains, and one undertaken by thousands of
walkers every year.

When two friends decided to walk the Dales Way
over a series of weekends they expected to complete
it within a year, but life got in the way. For one of
them, the Dales Way would remain an uncompleted
long distance footpath.

With details of the scenery, the natural history and
anecdotes about the walk, this book will give you a
true flavour of walking this often overlooked yet
delightful footpath. Light hearted but also darker at
times, Dawdling through the Dales, like all of Julia's
books, will make you laugh, but it might also make
you cry. It is a true tale of walking, divorce, betrayal,
depression and enduring friendship.

Cycling Through a Foreign Field
© Julia R May 2018
https://tinyurl.com/yc3rv2y7

In an overheated room in a sheltered housing complex
in Burnley there is a small, carved wooden box. The
box is a depository for memories, half remembered or
forgotten entirely. Inside this box are two life times
of old photographs, some sepia, some black and
white, known and unknown ancestors; and laid
carefully on top of them all sits a newspaper clipping,
faded and torn at the edges, over one hundred years
old now.

The clipping was taken from the Burnley Express
which in 1916 was running a regular feature of
Burnley families and the contributions they were
making to the First World War. The clipping shows
eight head and shoulder photographs of mother and
father and six of their sons. One son is in a reserved
occupation, one son is too young to fight. The other
four sons are in uniform, serving soldiers in the Great
War.

The occupant of this hot, stuffy little room and keeper
of this box of memories is a lady in her late eighties,
frail now and suffering from Alzheimer's Disease, her
memory is fading like the contents of the box. She is
my mother, Rose. The youngest son in the old
newspaper clipping is her father.

In spring 2018 my partner and I set out to cycle the
battlefields of Flanders and The Somme; to retrace
our forefathers' footsteps and to find out a little of
where they served, the conditions they endured and

what had become of them during the First World War.

By the same author but written under her previous name:

My Feet and Other Animals
© Julia R Merrifield 2003
https://tinyurl.com/y98fnuqx

When two friends planned a long distance walk on England's South West Coast Path they thought the toughest challenge would be the walking itself. But the biggest obstacles to be overcome were not the 630 miles of footpaths, or the soaring ascents and descents of the cliffs. They were the unforeseen factors that cannot be planned for but which transform a journey into an adventure. Factors such as a torn calf muscle, recalcitrant underwear, two days of torrential rain and gales, two weeks of the hottest July temperatures for years, high tech equipment designed to help but determined to hinder, the capriciousness of public transport and a host of B&Bs all competing for the title of Worst Accommodation in the West.

Walking Pembrokeshire with a Fruitcake
© Julia R Merrifield 2004
https://tinyurl.com/ycnuhgev

Two friends deliberated where to choose for their
next walking holiday. How about somewhere
different? How about somewhere exotic? How about
somewhere foreign? How about Wales? But with
countless people advising them where to walk that
summer and with neither of them speaking a word of
Welsh, had they made the right decision? On a hot
August day they set off to walk the 180 miles of the
Pembrokeshire Coast Path, starting from somewhere
unpronounceable and finishing at a little place called
Amroth, passing on the way lots more places they
would struggle to enunciate.

Wales, a proud land with a proud past; a land steeped
in history, a land of myths and magic, castles and
cromlechs, dragons and double consonants, male
voice choirs and Aled Jones. Follow their adventures
as they search for ice cream vans and a Welsh
dictionary.

Pedals, Panniers and Punctures
© Julia R Merrifield 2005
https://tinyurl.com/ybyfn8to

One woman, one bike, no backup and 1477 miles on a unique End to End adventure.

Since when did cycle touring become an extreme sport? Since it involved travelling by train. When one woman, more accustomed to long distance footpaths than long distance cycle rides, set out to cycle from Land's End to John o'Groats the first obstacle she faced was getting to the start. Between the start of her journey and the finish, 1477 miles later, she encountered not only ups and downs of terrain but mental and physical highs and lows as well.

Cycling the End to End is so much more than just sitting on something no bigger than, and as hard as, the sole plate of an iron and pedalling, as Julia was to discover. Every experience seemed to be about extremes: Cornish hills, Cheshire plains, busy Devon lanes, empty highland roads, downpours, droughts, smooth cycle tracks, hazardous cattle grids, psychedelic B&Bs and homely hostels. And when the terrain and the weather weren't against her the wildlife was: terrorising Labradors, formation herding sheep dogs, kamikaze squirrels, plagues of midges and road-senseless sheep.

With no backup, and just a bike and a puncture repair kit for company, that strangest of traveller, the lone female, set off to tackle the ultimate British cycle ride. If only she had got a pound for every time someone told her it was all downhill the other way she could have bought a lot more chocolate. As it was, sustained by copious quantities of tea and as much chocolate as she could carry she finally reached her wet and windswept goal.

Walking with Offa
© Julia R Merrifield 2006
https://tinyurl.com/yd73j3q8

Ever heard of a bloke called Offa? King of Mercia,
he instigated the building of a defensive dyke.
Twelve centuries later a long distance path was laid
out, roughly following the line of Offa's Dyke, and
thirty years later still two friends set out to walk it.

How difficult could it be, walking from one end of
Wales to the other? Loaded down with maps, guide
books and global positioning systems they were soon
to find out and only five minutes after leaving
Chepstow were monumentally lost! Soon they were
enjoying the scenery, watching the wildlife and
overdosing on dried apricots. Staying in haunted
English castles and heavenly Welsh guest houses they
made their way north.

Find me on Facebook:

For excerpts from my books, photos and more information.

Julia R May Books on Kindle & Kobo

https://www.facebook.com/JuliaRMayBooksOnKindle?ref_type=bookmark

If you like what I do – let people know. If you don't – shh! ☺

Printed in Great Britain
by Amazon

33877418R00120